CW01521803

This is the story of one spirit who originated from a distant star, travelled to planet earth in ethereal form and manifested as a human with the ancient Mayan, as an ambassador for mankind. From there a reincarnation was experienced in Atlantis, then subsequently in ancient Egypt, Greece and so on until the present time, where this story begins.

> Fear them not therefore: for there is nothing covered that shall
> not be revealed; and hid, that shall not be known.

> Matthew 10:26

Of course, one's life is affected by those around you and to some extent dictated to by events close to home and, as in every story, other characters must play their part. Heredity and environment also have an effect.

To,
Jane,
In Love e Light.

From,
Preston.

Star Child

Christine Marks

ATHENA PRESS
LONDON

ISBN 10-digit: 1 84748 107 8
ISBN 13-digit: 978 1 84748 107 8

First Published 2007 by
ATHENA PRESS
Queen's House, 2 Holly Road
Twickenham TW1 4EG
United Kingdom

Printed for Athena Press

This book is dedicated to all the physically, emotionally and mentally afflicted people in the world, who are screaming internally for help and understanding.

It is also for all the mothers who struggle to raise their families in the face of adverse circumstances and who wonder where they may have gone wrong without a guidance book to follow (such a book has yet to be written!).

And finally, to all the kids who wonder what their parents are thinking and long to know when they (the parents) are going to grow up!

Acknowledgements

Grateful thanks are given firstly to Helen who started me on my Spiritual pathway; to Barbara for the time spent typing from my handwritten notes; and to my family whose presence during my early years in the University of Life helped me to overcome my trials and tribulations at that time.

Also to Julie for her understanding of Spirit and all of its ramifications, for passing on the knowledge to me and giving support and advice while travelling the path. To Meg and Neris, for the very first introduction to a circle and the 'mechanics' of healing; Gina and Paul for subsequent awareness and development instruction; and Kathy, for suggesting that I should write.

To Joan, for her support and for allowing me to join the healing group and to Linda and Christopher for leading me on the search for connection with the angelic realm and further circle work.

To Hubby, for his help and encouragement and for the 'technical' bits.

Thanks also go to the publishers for accepting the manuscript for publication and of course to the proofreaders, without whose time this book would not have been completed.

My sincere gratitude and love are given to Spirit, whose prompting set me on the road to writing this book.

Foreword

ROBIN WINBOW is a dancer, choreographer, teacher in life sciences and Spirit and my mentor in helping me to understand the intricacies of Spirit work.

Robin has travelled extensively around the world. In former years he travelled across America and in more recent times to Israel, Spain and France, but mostly to Denmark, Sweden and Norway, working with Spirit as tutor, clairvoyant, clairaudient and trance.

May I recommend this book about personal and Spiritual involvement during their current lifetime on earth.

I first met Christine when she was wheeled into Grafton Road spiritualist church by her husband, Reg. On many occasions when I was working on the platform, I was drawn to them by messages from the Spirit world. There was always that aura of Spirituality as well as physical presence around them.

I was privileged to have them join my development workshop group and get to know them better. I say privileged because it was the first time ever that I had anyone special working and in a wheelchair. In fact I had two, both of them uplifting and exciting.

Christine has written this book relating to life, which will bring many memories of the past to some, and to others will lay bare the hardships of life before WWII and during it: a life without TV and many of our present luxuries.

Her memories rekindled one of mine – that of a theme song to a film:

> I know where I'm going…
> And I know who's going with me…

I know who I love…
But the dear Lord know who I'll marry…[1]

In this book, Christine and Reg have endeavoured to show the way that they found and developed their own Spirituality alongside the reality of their own physical lives and understanding of the grand vista of life within the continuing existence of being, created by the living force that we call God.

Their meditations and exercises are for you to explore and experience, for you to follow and digest, so that you too may open that Spiritual pathway of understanding and find out not only *who* you are, but also *what* you are and the realities that exist within reality.

---

[1] The song was also the title of a 1945 film set in Scotland with Wendy Hillier (1912–2003). The film title *I Know Where I'm Going* was originally sung by Kathleen Ferrier (1912–1953) of 'Blow the Wind Southerly' fame. The first two lines are as in the song. The second two lines are Robin's own rendering and reflects that Spirit knows what will happen.

Preface

Hi! Thank you for dipping into this book and reading through some of its pages. It embraces what a newcomer to Spirituality might experience, plus that which an ardent traveller has experienced. There's some philosophy and a few new thoughts.

It is a true-life story, warts and all! It traces the life of me, the author, from birth and through some seventy years, up to the present time. Some of the names have been changed to protect the identities of various people, but where they are known to have passed to Spirit or in the cases of very good friends, the real names are used to honour them. To keep the story flowing and in as correct a chronological order as possible, some events which in fact occurred simultaneously have had to be written as separate issues for clarity. It details some horrific occurrences, (which some of you might find familiar from your own lives), including a plane crash and my disability, but all can be put down to hard lessons in the earlier years of the University of Life. Things get better in places as time goes on, and certainly for me during the last decade, in which I have developed a whole new understanding of how Spirit works.

If you look at your own life experiences, you might see several events that have either come to a satisfactory conclusion or have had a knock-on effect. One needs to remember that wounds *do* heal, but the scars always remain to remind you.

In the University of Life there is no pass or fail. We all achieve a distinction in one degree or another, according to our own life experiences; we make of it as we will. Indeed, we all have free will and it is how we assess each daily situation and the actions we take, and even what we think, that determine what will happen next.

Think of a pebble dropped into a pond and the ripples expanding across the surface of the water. The ripples strike the far side and rebound back towards the centre, but don't stop there. The initial wave has diminished and is counteracted by the rebounding wave, which may be small or large depending on the surface and contour of the pond's edge. Such is life – our actions and our thoughts all have an action and *re*action, which may be received as a good thing or one that isn't really wanted or expected.

Read on, think on, and enjoy, or even cry if you have the need to! Sympathies I do not need, and this is not a book about 'poor me' as I have accepted and overcome my difficulties and there are those in the world who are far worse off than me. My only wish is that some of the words written in this book give you inspiration, that you can look at all that life has thrown at you, and hope that you can assess each situation as it arises. Accept it, and I hope that you too can find the path to Spirituality and happiness.

The Force is out there… Look for it.

Happy hunting!

Christine Marks

Contents

Introduction

The Gold-Encircled Cross and Star

A circle is a shape without a beginning or an end, but the line has a thickness, therefore an inner and an outer surface. The centre is an infinitesimal dot surrounded by the whole: the 'I am'. It is there but, unless it is large enough, it cannot be seen. Such is Spirit within each of us and indeed within all things that we can see in this materialistic world, be they vegetable, mineral, gases of the air or waters of the sea.

The **outer circle** of the pictogram represents the energy of life that comes to earth from the cosmos via the sun's rays. Akhenaten, in bringing the one God to the people of Egypt in his time, recognised this fact, and in the paintings of Tutenkamun, his son, seated on the throne with his wife facing him, the rays of the sun above them each have a hand on the lower end. I have interpreted these as being the hand of God touching all things.

The Dogon, an African tribe, has had information passed down through their tribal stories of them having come to earth via the sun, from Sirius, the Dog Star. They also have the knowledge – long before astronomers recently established the fact – that there are two stars/planets circling the Dog Star in orbits that are at right angles to each other.

The **golden cross** is an ancient emblem, and includes the Hammer of Thor. In this instance, the cross would be depicted upside down, suspended by the end of the handle or shaft. In no way does it represent the dark side of life. The cross is of course used in churches around the world by various Christian religions.

The **cross and circle** configuration is used by the healers of the White Eagle organisation on completion of a healing session

As above
COSMIC

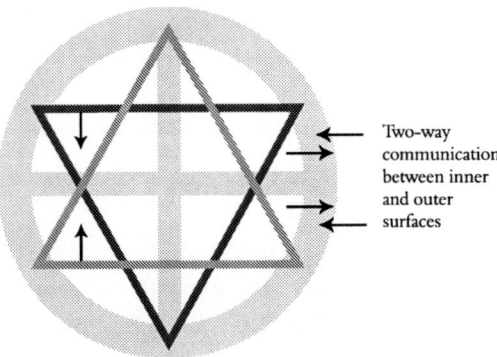

Two-way
communication
between inner
and outer
surfaces

CELL
So Below
In the centre of the two
intertwined pyramids
and of the cross is:
Acceptance/change

Material Plane

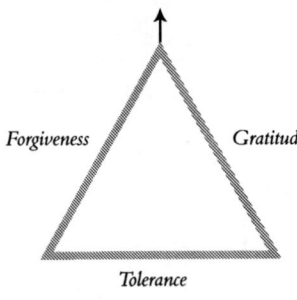

Forgiveness

Gratitude

Tolerance

Spiritual Plane

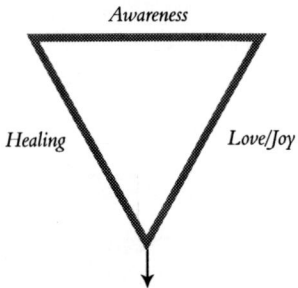

Awareness

Healing

Love/Joy

to seal and close down the patient, and is formed by hand movements across the patient's back.

The cross and circle together are also used by the American Indians. The circle is symbolic of Mother Earth, with the cross representing the four directions, north, south, east and west, as well as the elements fire, water, air and metal/earth. The centre of the cross indicates the burning of their campfire, the light of Spirit.

The fire also identifies change. Everything changes; it does not die and disappear for ever. The wood burning on the fire changes to ash, the ash returns to the earth and helps to invigorate new life, and so the cycle continues. The cross and circle is also shown on the headband of White Eagles' feathered headdresses.

The **star** is representative of two three-sided pyramids: one with the apex pointing upwards, the other with the apex pointing downwards, superimposed one on the other. The upward-pointing pyramid represents the earth, the material side of life and all that there is. The downward pyramid represents the whole of the cosmos, the universe, the unseen and the Spiritual side of life and the male and female aspects. When superimposed and merged, the two are sometimes known as a merkabah, which, according to the rules of Melchizadek, rotates at nine-tenths the speed of light and is used in some advanced metaphysical meditations.

The gleaming white star, also known as the Star of David, is also used separately by the White Eagle Lodge, and during the healing part of their service. Members of the congregation are asked to meditate on this star, bringing the life force energy into them using the star as a conduit, for the golden white light.

There is a correlation between the star, cross and circle configuration that encompasses time and space. The star is an object that is at a distance, (*di-stance*):

di: the separation of two parts of a whole, as in 'dissect'

stance: the actual being in a place, of either part

Time is a man-made element to identify a distance travelled within established parameters, and light years, the distance travelled by light within a given time frame. This raises the possibility that the stars in the heavens at night are not in fact there at all, and what we see is simply the residual light from their explosion which may have occurred eons ago. How many stars are really up there, then, and are there stars whose light has yet to reach our senses?

As above, the macrocosm...

...so below, the microcosm

The above description of the encircled cross and star relate primarily to the greater being, the cosmos, the universe, the macrocosm and to Mother Earth herself. In its own right it is a model of a smaller entity. The atmosphere above us is the covering membrane of protection, as is the mantle on which we all reside. It stops harmful rays from the sun destroying the earth; it protects us from the small meteorites that bombard the earth; it allows the passage of electrical impulses, radio waves and light, to pass through to the cosmos and even our thoughts. The mantle, the bit we all stand upon, protects us from the molten core of the earth.

This can also be applied to an individual cell. A single cell has a membrane covering the nucleus. It has a thickness, (the outer circle of our emblem) which again gives protection against unwanted forces, but allows the passage of intelligence on a two-way journey. It also has the ability to attach itself to other cells. In his book *The Biology of Belief*, Dr Bruce Lipton postulates that the membrane of a cell has a brain. It governs and directs the working of the cell.

Where is the brain in the earth's membrane? It is the brain in all of the inhabitants of the earth, human and animal alike and is situated generally within the first few feet (relatively speaking) of the surface of the earth and is in all of our heads! At the moment, we live in communities of incompatible people, thinking only of ourselves as individuals, as races mingled and living side by side with other races, of different creeds, religions and beliefs, of nation adjacent to nation. There is no real compatibility with one's neighbours. All think and act separately. As cells in your body, this would cause emotional and mental disturbances. It would attract like to like. It would cause small cancerous cells, which would grow, as diseases grow. *Dis-ease!* So it is with planet earth, your brain, like a single cell, controls your destiny. Relax, enjoy, nation to nation. Not only those with separate boundaries, but also those that live intermingled with others. Be at peace with yourself, with one another. The world as a whole is able to repair itself given the chance. It will get better for the good of all. When the outward emanations from the planet to the cosmos are of a higher vibration, this will attract better and even higher vibrations. We would have cured the dis-ease!

When all can think alike for the highest good together, then we will be able to communicate with other cosmic 'cells'. There is also intelligence in the plant kingdom, otherwise how do they know how and when to grow within their seasons? Like the single cell, the earth also has a similar 'construction'.

The cross of the four directions of the emblem symbolises not only four directions, but all directions. Inside the membrane, a multitude of activity ensues. Gathering of information, decisions made, and two-way communication with adjacent cells.

The star can be interpreted as follows. The upward-pointing triangle can now represent the attributes that are directed by thought, by your own direction, i.e. tolerance, forgiveness, gratitude. The downward-pointing triangle can represent the aspirations which come from a Spiritual level, i.e. awareness, healing, love/joy. In the very centre of the emblematic cross is the value of acceptance of change.

All seven attributes mingle and can pass (communicate) from the nucleus of a single cell to other adjoining cells. One definition of this could be the expression – collective intelligence, where what one knows, all know. This also happens in the animal kingdom where, for argument's sake, when one elephant finds a new waterhole, the rest of the herd immediately knows of its whereabouts without vocal communication. Think of one of your organs – say the liver. In its entirety it functions without outside help, but each single cell is working together with others so that the liver continues its designed function. The liver in its entirety has a membrane and it also communicates with other parts of the anatomy.

If you are feeling down, try this simple exercise. Imagine a single cell, anywhere in your body; it is a small circle. Now place a smile in it for a mouth and two specks for the eyes. You now have a smile within you!

Spread that smile to all of the adjacent cells and spread it as far as you want to. Why stop with just yourself, why not pass it on to others?

1

The First Years

I am now three score years and ten, so I'll start, like all good stories do, at the beginning.

I was born in the front parlour of my grandmother's house in a small village in Sussex where the rolling South Downs sweep almost to the sea. The property is one of a pair of semi-detached red-brick houses, with three rows of red tiles on the otherwise grey roof. My grandfather and his brother built it several years before I was born, and they made the bricks in the brickfields they owned in a nearby lane. Before they married, Gran was working in Goodwood House as a laundry maid, rising to head laundry maid as time went by. I was fortunate enough to have this fact verified on a visit to that great house, when the staff looked up the details in the house records for me. Gran and Granddad used to travel on a tandem bicycle to and from Midhurst, Gran's birthplace. Granddad originally lived in Cocking.

The house had a trellis around the back door, and Granddad used to tend to all the rambling roses climbing over it and also the flowers that were planted in the borders. Mum and her sisters had to help Granddad cover the bricks with tarpaulins to protect them from the rain and frost, a gruelling task, there being no brothers to help them. At some point, Granddad had an accident while leading the horse that was used to pull the cart loaded with bricks from where they were made to the place where they were stored. The horse fell on him and broke his back and this put paid to his working career. When he recovered somewhat, he then had to resort to walking with two sticks. He was, however, able to tend to his garden, and as a small child I remember being allowed to help pick the soft fruit. He grew all manner of fruits and vegetables and the garden was kept meticulously neat and tidy.

With Granddad being out of action, as it were, Gran had to take in washing for a living. After it had been boiled in the gas-fired copper, it was put through an old-fashioned mangle, and then Gran had to iron all the laundry with a flat iron heated on the black range in the kitchen. It was my job to deliver all the brown paper parcels, neatly tied with string, around the village on foot after school, and also to run errands.

On the corner of the adjacent street was a shoe repairer who worked in a wooden shed. Granddad liked to go there, smoke his pipe and talk to the man while he worked repairing the shoes. In a cage just at the shed opening was a green parrot that had a fine repertoire, including a few choice words!

I also remember that the post used to be delivered by a lady driving a dogcart! There was also a gypsy who called, selling watercress at the door. I was always sent into another room, as I couldn't stop giggling when he called. The poor man had a cleft palette and I used to go into hysterics.

At some time about then we moved into the house next door to Gran and Granddad.

I was given a dog, a black-and-white collie mongrel that I called 'Boy' or, more often than not, 'Boysee'. He went every-where with me, and it was up to me to make sure that he didn't upset Granddad's garden too much with his digging. I remember going to see my dad playing football in the local park, and Boysee would accompany me and run up and down the sideline when we were shouting to egg the team on.

Mother also cleaned other people's houses to help bring in some money and so Gran looked after me most of the time, as I must have been only about four or five then.

Dad took out indentures to become a carpenter with some urging from mother, a job that he became very good at eventually.

Home life was becoming stressful for me, as Mum and Dad were not at all compatible, what with the raised voices, constant arguments, and flying dinner plates! I must have been about five when Dad took me to the pictures to see Snow White, shortly followed by Bambi, Pinocchio, and Dumbo. It was a special treat for me, as it probably was for a great number of children in that age group, with Lyons ice cream in a paper cup with a little wooden spoon. Not that much different from today really, except that all the containers and spoons are plastic, while the ice cream is nowhere as delicious as it was then.

When my sister was born she suffered with rickets, and Mum had a job trying to find the right diet for her. She had to go to hospital about five miles away for what was known then as 'sunlight treatment' and wear dark glasses. I think this must have been ultra-violet treatment (these days used for SAD, or Seasonal Affective Disorder). Mum had to walk with the pushchair both ways as she didn't have enough money for the bus fare. Time went on, and when I was seven Mum and Dad divorced.

It was wartime now and Dad joined the navy. He was mainly stationed around the British coastline, although I'm sure he must have travelled further afield at some point. We did find out much later that he had been wounded; he was a gunner on deck at the time, but more of that when you read about psychic messages.

After he left home I was not to see my dad again for another twenty-odd years. Mum was quite adamant about us not seeing him. Meanwhile, he had met and married another woman, so he had to support his new family and it was left up to Mum to try and make ends meet for us. We had very little and Mum seemed to be working most of the time. Gran made sure that my sister and I had a hot meal every day and generally looked after us as a mother should.

Around that time I recall having an infestation of massive boils all over my arms and legs; those that were close to each other were called carbuncles. They were so painful! I walked in my sleep, stuttered and had the most awful nightmares. I hated school and was always being pushed and bullied by the boys. With this and the life in general at home I was not a very happy soul. My escape from reality was to play and talk to my imaginary friends and of course I had my dog as companion, when he wasn't wandering around the village looking for a lady friend.

My sister was sent to what Mum called 'camp school', (probably what is now known as summer camp) for character and physical development to build up her strength as she was very weak, thin and shut-in on herself. She was a timid child and Mum thought the experience would teach her self-reliance. She was a changed person that came back home. I remember that Mum did not go to see her while she was away; she thought it better not to as my sister would have wanted to come home. Besides, there were insufficient funds for visiting. I felt sorry for her and used to write her letters, describing what was going on. Mum had a few boyfriends and became pregnant again and this time she had a little boy called Billy, with beautiful blue eyes and a mass of curly hair. We all loved him – he was like a ray of sunshine in the house. We used to sing him to sleep with 'The Skye Boat Song'. When he was a year old he contracted pneumonia, and after a little while he died. It was a terrible time. We were all traumatised and it took ages to get over his passing. How we grieved for him.

Mum stabilized her friendship with a merchant seaman called Albert, (although he was more often than not called 'Bow'). Before they went out together he had lodged with Gran. He had been a foundling on a doorstep in London within the sound of Bow bells, hence the nickname. He and Mum initially corresponded a lot. Eventually they married and went to London to see the musical *Oklahoma*, leaving us, of course, in the care of Gran. Well, they wouldn't want us tagging along on this occasion, would they?

Bow was away a lot on oil tankers and was even on the *San Demetrio* when she was torpedoed and caught fire. This boat was the subject of a film starring Stanley Baker. The tanker was hit but did not sink. The crew abandoned her and escaped in the lifeboats, only to be able to return to her some days later, re-board her, put the fires out and get home safely.

Our lives and Mum's were a lot happier for a while and as I wasn't getting on too well at my school, Mum arranged for me to go to a private school which enabled me to catch up and become a little more confident, even though I was still somewhat withdrawn and shy. I spent a fair bit of time at Mum's workplace and was allowed to play in the garden during the summer months and school holidays. Her employers had a large fishpond with water lilies and koi carp and a beautiful garden with all kinds of plants, shrubs and colourful flowers. Just as with Granddad's garden there were also many fruit trees and soft fruit bushes and peas and beans which I was allowed to help pick, eating more than my fair share at the same time, I might add! Mum spent many an hour preparing the fruit and making various jams for storage. There was also a Wendy house, not like the fragile plastic and canvas ones you see today, but one made of timber, with a thatched roof, proper windows and a door. I was allowed to unlock the door with a key, and inside there were table, chairs, a dresser with a china tea set and pretty curtains at the windows. I loved it in there; I was away from reality and could talk and play with my imaginary friends as much as I liked.

With the war going on all around us, Granddad built an air raid shelter under the apple tree in his garden. We didn't like using it much as it smelt of wet earth, lime and of the occasional cat that visited it. When it rained there were puddles on the floor from which even the duckboards didn't really give total protection and it took for ever to try and clean them up, always leaving a muddy slush at the bottom which did eventually dry out, until the next downpour. During the overhead raids, Granddad would walk up and down the garden path waving his sticks at the aircraft dog fighting above and cursing and swearing at them. I guess that was probably where I learnt a few new words outside of the school curriculum!

Like the rest of the children and some adults, we had to carry our gasmasks everywhere with us, and we did get used to the sirens sounding when a raid was imminent. One day, I was sent on an errand to the local shops during a raid, when I heard and saw a German plane zooming down to rooftop height. The pilot started to machinegun the people in the street, me included! I did nothing more than dive into an alleyway between two of the houses and crouch down against the wall, shaking like a leaf. I guess I was crying, too (but I cannot quite remember that bit) and stayed there until the all-clear sounded.

I hated the doodlebugs too, as you never knew where they were going to come down. You were safe all the time that you could hear them, but once the engine stopped you never knew which direction they were going. In some respects they were more terrifying than the bombing raids. One night, one came over and Mum called me from a deep sleep and, in my haste to get downstairs, I fell from the top to the bottom. I was black and blue all over, but did I get any sympathy? Of course not!

At this time we also had an indoor shelter, if you can call it such, built like a steel cage with a solid top that served as our dining table in the parlour. It wouldn't have served any protection from a direct hit, but would have given a little protection from falling debris through a near miss. We children would crouch under the table on cushions to make it as comfortable as possible, leaving Mum and an aunt to squeeze under as best they could. What a sight it must have been with their bottoms stuck up in the air on the outside! The railway line wasn't too far away and more often than not, was a target for the bombers as well as Ford and Tangmere airfields. The Windmill Bridge, down the road by the Windmill pub, had an ack-ack anti-aircraft gun emplacement each side, so we could quite easily hear the crump of the shells as they exploded above.

Although we were on the coast, we did receive evacuees from London; a woman and her daughter were billeted with us. When it was time for them to leave, the precocious little girl played up and wanted to have the precious doll that my stepdad had sent to me from America. Mother made me give up my Rosy, saying that they had lost everything in the London air raids, and that I shouldn't be so selfish.

A lot of soldiers of different nationalities were billeted around the village, and I believe that a fair old time was had by one and all, as I can remember them climbing over the back garden fences from one house to another. At the time Mum was in the local darts team at The Windmill and had more than a few admirers. She seemed to prefer men's company to that of other women. The Americans brought nylons, tins of food and other commodities that were not readily available in the shops. The Canadians were there also and my Aunt Doff married one of them and sailed to Canada on one of the liners that transported a whole bunch of war brides. They lived in Quebec for a few years but she came back after a while, as the winters were too harsh and long for her.

I started helping mother in the house, cleaning my room at first, but I was soon elevated to doing the whole house. As I got a bit older, I had to do the washing up and also learnt to cook the

Sunday roast with all the trimmings, so it wasn't long before I was also preparing the vegetables every day. Later on I was taught how to make cakes. During the war everything was in short supply, with the inevitable queues for limited food that was available through rationing. This was supplemented by eggs from Grand-dad's chickens and what he would grow in the garden. He also kept rabbits so we fared better than most.

Eventually the war ended and life went on as normally as could be expected. I was allowed to go and see my other Gran who lived in the Cornfield Cottages near Wick. These were farm workers' houses surrounded by fields where I used to play with my aunt who was four years younger than me. I loved going there as Gran used to spoil us by giving us a full fried breakfast in bed. She only used a primus stove to cook the breakfast on, but managed to feed the whole family by using the main range for the roast dinners and cakes.

Sometimes we were allowed to go with Granddad to The Globe, the pub in Wick or The Locomotive nearby. As youngsters we had to sit outside eating crisps and drinking fizzy lemonade while we could hear granddad banging away on the piano inside. He was somewhat tone-deaf, and quite riotous at times, but we all had a good laugh. Gran Wells used to read the tea leaves around the tea table on Sundays. We would sit around munching salad and ham sandwiches, followed by winkles, homemade cakes and laugh, tease and have a good old gossip. She also liked having her 'fortune' told and would visit a woman in Littlehampton and take Auntie Maureen with her, who used to sit outside because she was nervous at the thought of being told what might be in store for her. Interestingly, her grandson today is quite psychic in his own right.

Mum used to bring home some of her employer's daughter's clothes for me. They were awful! Most were either too loose around the middle or too long at the hem, being at least two sizes too big for me. The gymslips in particular were too long and the blouses too long in the sleeves. Some could be taken up, as Mum couldn't afford new clothes for me at the rate I was growing. I started secondary school, but I still didn't like it much, although there were some lessons that I could get on with such as games, music, history, writing essays and cookery. Maths, algebra and some of the science studies were far beyond my comprehension. I remember having to make a cookery apron for myself in domestic science/needlework and managed to prick my fingers with the needle and get blood all over the white material!

I eventually got myself a paper round and was out in all weathers around the Sea Estate and the village. I had to go to the newsagents early to make up my own round and then deliver the papers, which I did for four years before going to school. Having reached puberty during my early teens with no knowledge of 'the menses', I woke up in a dreadful state one day, covered in blood and in pain. I called Mum who proceeded to give me a telling off!

I was now doing most of the chores around the house, cleaning, washing and ironing the gym slips with a damp cloth to put the pleats in, the socks and blouses for my sister and myself. This included all the underclothes and shoes, so my time was pretty well taken up before we went to school. Mum was never a housekeeper and didn't do a thing in her own home; I guess she thought that she had enough of it where she worked. With all this going on, I didn't have time or chance to make firm friends with my schoolmates, so I would save up what pocket money I could earn and take myself off to the pictures. Providing I had done the chores, Mum didn't seem to mind what I got up to, or where I went, providing I kept out of trouble.

At one time, as I had a reasonable ear for music, Mum thought I should have piano lessons from one of the teachers from school. I couldn't get my head around the musical score; it made no sense to me whatsoever. So I skipped class and went out with Lilly, one of my friends. This soon got back to Mother's ears and guess what? Yes, that's right – I was in trouble again. By now I felt that my place in life was as a domestic for my mother!

Around this time, my stepdad modernised the house. A hot water tank was put in so that we didn't have to use the gas copper for hot water and the kettles. We had a Hoover so that we didn't have to rely on a dustpan and brush to sweep up. The old black range went out and a new Rayburn was installed. Mum asked me to help her make a couple of new rugs with the ready-cut kits. We sat opposite each other working towards the middle; they were pale green, beige, and pink. There was no television in those days, but we enjoyed the radio programmes such as *Workers' Playtime* at midday, *Woman's Hour* in the afternoon, plays and *Children's Hour*. Some of the other programmes were *Dick Barton, Special Agent*, *Paul Temple*, and *The Huggets*, with entertainers such as Joyce Grenfell, Elsie and Doris Waters, Gracie Fields, and Vera Lynn, to name but a few. Gran had a wind-up gramophone and several seventy-eight records. It was a great treat to go next door some Sunday afternoons and into the front parlour and play them. She had all of Snow White's monologue and songs, Gene Autrey, Roy Rogers, Bing Crosby, Ann Shelton, Deanna Durban, Paul Robeson, The Ink Spots and many more. My aunt said that I could have the records when Granddad and Gran passed away, but she forgot when the time came and gave them to the work-house in East Preston. I didn't begrudge her decision as they would have many hours of enjoyment from them. Several of the records, if they were still around somewhere today, would be real classics and collectors' items.

I loved all the westerns at the cinema; the Indians all had a bad time of it, as history has also confirmed. It is gratifying that they have a voice which is heard these days and my sympathies have always been with them. Mum said at one time that she never forgot the *Buffalo Bill Wild West Show* when it came to South-ampton. She really enjoyed it, but I don't think I went as I have no recollection of it.

One of my aunts was a trained caterer and always made our birthday cakes and fancies for tea. She would write our name on the cake, which we thought was rather special. I thought it was lovely to have an aunt who was so clever. As I used to bite my nails a lot (a sure sign of insecurity) this aunt also said that she would buy me a manicure set if I managed to grow my nails. I never could, so that put the spoke in that little wheel!

I would take myself off to the downs or the woods with Boy-see, and enjoy the peace of the surroundings just listening to the birds, the wind in the grass or the trees, and watching the bees, insects, and dragonflies by the water. The wild flowers were varied and riotous with colour.

Looking back, I remember going to Sunday school, where we

each received a coloured text from the Bible every week and we had to stick it onto a card. Our Sunday school teacher, Miss Summers and her brother, lived in a big house near the sea front. My Aunt Dolly used to live in as their maid and was responsible for doing the housework on her own: the cooking, washing and ironing, and all for very little money. She worked there from my early childhood until she reached retirement age. Once a year after Sunday school as a special treat, Aunt Dolly came round and served us with sandwiches and tea, wearing her little starched frilly hat and apron. She worked very hard for all those years and had nothing at the end of it. No gratuity or pension other than that provided by the state. She suffered terribly with arthritis and painful knees in her old age.

She would come round to Gran's house on her afternoons off and do embroidery. She did some beautiful work and I still have several pieces. One night, while she was still in service during the war, a bomb came through her bedroom ceiling, went through the floor and ended up in the basement – yet it didn't explode. Poor Aunty Dolly, her nerves were shot to pieces. She never really got over the shock and was a bundle of nerves to her dying day.

The Early Teens

I left school at fifteen as Mum felt there was no point in my staying on, besides which, the family allowance of half a crown wasn't much and she needed me to bring in a full wage. I got a job with a local builder, living with his wife and family in East Preston and doing the housework and cooking and taking the children out in the afternoon. I would give them their tea upon return, get them washed and changed for bed. My hours were from nine in the morning until six in the evening – every day except Sundays. I then had to go home and do the housework for Mum. Out of my wages I was allowed to keep about four shillings' pocket money. Mum had the rest for my keep.

I had a boyfriend who lived across the fields at Poling, who used to take me for walks across the fields to catch rabbits. I was always amazed that he was so quiet and slow that he was able to crawl right up to a rabbit and catch it by the ears. Across the brooks there was a maze of wild flowers and I learnt where the wild orchids, best watercress and mushrooms grew. Blackberries were plentiful, as were the chestnuts. It was a lovely area in the spring and summer months, and I always enjoyed my escape from reality, when I could leave all the cares of the day behind. This boyfriend came from a large family and I still manage to keep in touch with one of his sisters, even though we parted and he met someone else.

I gave up the job with the builder and went to Surrey for a live-in job at a hotel, looking after the owners' children, a son and daughter. This was a lot easier than the long hours in my previous job. Once, one of the kitchen staff started to get too friendly and after he came into my bedroom and sat on the bed one night, I kept the bedroom door locked! However, while there, I made friends with a woman and her young daughter and although I returned to Rustington soon afterwards, I asked her to keep in touch with me. She wrote to me having decided that she would like to come to Sussex and asked if she could stay with me until she found a job. Mum was constantly in a temper over something or other and I couldn't pluck up the courage to ask her, so when the woman and her daughter turned up on the doorstep, Mum flew into another rage and sent them packing. I felt awful and suffered terrible pangs of conscience afterwards and hoped that they managed to find somewhere. I never heard from them again. Frankly, I don't blame them!

Life and time went on as they do, and I ended up with a job in a photographic developing and printing company in Church Street, Littlehampton, next door to the Palladium Cinema, opposite the church. The cinema has long gone now, as have many others such as The Regent, (more commonly known as 'The Fleapit') opposite the railway station and the Odeon, where Curry's is now situated. There were always plenty of films to go and see. Also, in those days, there were always two major films showing on any particular day.

At last I had found a job that I really enjoyed. Real work, not housekeeping or looking after children! (I know – some would say that looking after children is more that real work and I'd agree, but you know what I mean).

I had to collect the films for developing from all the chemists in town where the holidaymakers had deposited them to be processed. I learnt how to wash and dry the films, sort them by the individual customer's identification, and deliver them back to the correct chemist. I was taught how to do the developing and printing processes, trim the edges and occasionally tint them, colour films not being widely available in those days. There was a lot to do as the films were in great demand, especially as most were on either a same day turn around or, if we were lucky, the following day. Enlargements took a little bit longer, but other staff were responsible for those. It was a time-consuming process and of course quite antiquated by today's standards when it's all done within the hour, or if you have your own printer, even quicker!

I enjoyed the work, but as most of you will have experienced, there's always someone at work you cannot get on with. I was still unhappy at home which reflected in my attitude and demeanour and I remained reserved when compared to the other girls, who had a better relationship with their parents.

Growing Up Fast

At seventeen I went to the cinema as usual and the usherette showed me to my seat. I don't remember what film was showing. As my eyes got used to the gloom I became aware that I was sitting in a row of sailors stationed a couple of miles away at Ford Naval Air Station, HMS *Peregrine*. I sat next to the man who was destined to be my future husband. We got chatting and – well, you know what sailors are – it turned out that he hadn't been in the Fleet Air Arm very long and that he had only just been posted to Ford straight from initial training.

He was working on various planes such as the rare Barracuda. He was also working on Attackers, the first jet naval aircraft, and on Fireflies. One incident he told me about soon after we had met concerned his torch. After he had helped a chief petty officer who was familiarising him with the aircraft to ready a Firefly for flight, he realised that his torch hadn't been returned to him after the pre-flight check. This is an inspection that every aircraft is subjected to, to ensure that the plane is flight-worthy. He related the following exchange:

'Hey chief, you got my torch?'

'No!'

'Where is it then?'

'It's in the bucket.'

'Where's the bucket?'

A strange look came over him and he dashed off to the office to phone air traffic control. The crash crew were alerted, and the pilot was instructed to fly over low, slow and on a straight course so that ground crew could check with binoculars that the landing gear was properly secured in the down position, the pilot confirming he had the correct indicator lights in the cockpit. The Firefly landed safely, and the bucket was found in the wheel well, spectacularly mangled, but without damage to the aircraft. His torch? It was fine and still in a working condition.

While at Ford, a fleet review took place, and all the aircraft in the Naval Air Service flew into Ford for the event. On the day of the fly past over the fleet, every single plane participated. The runways were so full that those at front had to be helped with RATOG (rocket-assisted take-off gear) in order to become airborne.

We started going out together regularly and I took him home to meet Mother. Needless to say, she didn't care for him very much. If we went for a walk she would follow behind, never letting us out of her sight. Of course, we did manage to give her the slip now and again so that we could be alone: we were in love and not ashamed of the fact.

The time came when Reg had to go on a course. He couldn't tell me so I thought he was seeing someone else. I didn't know where he had gone – so much for true love! I didn't see him for some time and started dating another fellow. He did come back to Ford eventually but I was so mad that he hadn't written to me and let me know where he was. I decided I shouldn't get too serious about him, but I couldn't help myself. However, I felt – no, *knew* – that he was the person that I wanted to marry. We had a lot in common, shared the same sense of humour, liked the same things and had the same interests. We were sure that we wanted to marry, but both of our parents were against it. We were only nineteen at this point, and found that we couldn't wait any longer, so Reg took me up to Farnham to meet his parents. They didn't like me at all, and his mum told me she wanted something better for her son: she thought I wasn't good enough for him! Nothing changes in the world, does it?

Needless to say I walked out and Reg followed and we went to live at my mother's. Reg was then stationed for a short time at Lee-on-Solent, on HMS *Daedalus*, working as an aircraft fitter and rigger on Firefly aircraft, and was operating with plenty of flying hours to his credit, with 771X flight on special exercises. He told me that on one flight they seemed to be taking a bit longer to fly from the Weymouth area back to Lee-on-Solent. It was foggy on the ground and all that could be seen was the tops of the largest hills and high radio masts. Reg saw a particularly high tower and asked the pilot if it was Blackpool Tower. The pilot said 'Drat!' (or words to that effect), and turned sharply left. It turned out that he had recognised the Eiffel Tower! They were well and truly off course but as they got nearer the channel coastline, the fog cleared and they made a late landfall at Lee-on-Solent.

Reg and I arranged to get married that March but on the day of his move back to Ford he had all of his savings and pay stolen, so we started married life with very little cash. I had five pounds – just enough for the ring – and we went on the bus to Worthing Registrars to be wed with two friends who were to be the witnesses. It was raining and I was a bundle of nerves and could hardly speak, but we managed to get through the service without too much difficulty and came out into the sunshine. A gypsy came to us at the bus stop where we were waiting to catch a bus back to Rustington and gave us her blessing, saying that we would have a happy and long life together.

On arrival back home, my aunt had made us a wedding cake and provided a lovely spread. Reg had got in a small barrel of beer although he didn't drink at that time. My sister however, did, had too much and was sick in the front garden! Mother as usual went into one of her rages and broke the camera so we ended up without any wedding photos. However, we were man and wife now, had our future lives together and nothing else seemed to matter, although this did cause a few embarrassing moments later in life when friends wanted to see photos of that happy day!

When our daughter was six months old, Reg got a posting to Lossiemouth on the coast of the Moray Firth in Morayshire, northern Scotland, not too far from Findhorn, a Spiritualist centre and retreat as it turned out. We were not Spiritually aware then, however, and not aware of its connotations. The Rustington district nurse offered to help me travel to London on the train to Kings Cross. I had never really been far out of Sussex, so I found it a bit daunting, taking a young baby and my entire luggage on the Aberdonian overnight express train to Aberdeen. Nurse Ryan was a real brick and made sure I caught all the right connections and was settled into the right compartment of the train. She really was a good soul and often helped people beyond the call of duty as a district nurse.

It was a long journey and on arrival at Aberdeen a stranger kindly helped me with all my chattels. I couldn't see Reg anywhere, although he had promised to meet me. Then I spotted him disappearing over one of the platform bridges going in the opposite direction. I couldn't make him hear me what with all the general noise, bustle and steam issuing from the trains. Luckily I managed to get another sailor to call after him and then leg it to bring him back and reunite us. Then we were onto another train from a different platform and on to Lossiemouth. I think that the total journey took something like eighteen hours, so we arrived very tired and weary. It was here that Reg worked on Sturgeons, a two-engine light bomber and also the Admiral's personal plane, a Dehavilland Dove, an eight-seater passenger plane with two engines. Shortly after that he worked in the blacksmith's shop in the aircraft repair section. It was here he joined the naval fencing team and learned to use the foil, épée, and sabre.

We found lodgings with an elderly lady in a fisherman's cottage backing onto the Moray Forth. We were soon to find out what the northern storms were like as the waves actually crashed over the sea wall onto the roof of the cottage. Not just spray, but waves of solid water! The cottage itself was unique to us; there was just the one room with a fireplace opposite an alcove where the bed was. This alcove had wooden planks enclosing it to a height of about three feet. The bed was made up of several mattresses and feather eiderdowns thrown into the well, so when we got into bed we just sank down together – bliss! The alcove had a curtain to enclose it, and so we were as snug as bugs in a rug! Between the bed alcove and the fireplace were a small table, two dining chairs, an armchair, a two-seater settee and the cot. Through a doorway was the kitchen area, with a tin bath hanging on a hook behind the door. The cooker was a Belling two-ring electric stove with an oven underneath, barely big enough to roast a pigeon let alone a chicken!

We stayed there for some time until the landlady found out that I was pregnant again – she wasn't having any of that under *her* roof! We managed to find alternative digs across the other side of town, overlooking the bay at a river estuary. The landlady here was a dream. Ginnie was her name and she originated from Aberdeen. It took a while to get accustomed to her dialect but after a little time I picked up the brogue myself, much to the amusement of those back down south when I eventually returned. She had a son, Alex, living with her, and a small grandson. Alex was a fisherman and would spend most nights out fishing on a trawler along with the rest of the fleet. Lossiemouth was a fishing port, on the North Sea beyond the Moray forth. The fish couldn't be any fresher, and we had the choice of several varieties. Occasionally Reg would go down to the depot of an evening to gut and clean the catch and ice them up prior to despatch on the train down south.

We settled in nicely here. When winter came it turned out to be the worst they had had in that area for several years. This was 1954–55, and most of northern Scotland was cut off from supplies. The Naval Air Station had to operate day and night in shifts for some weeks to keep a runway clear to allow relief planes to land and take off, air-dropping vital equipment and food to outlying villages and towns throughout the whole of the area. In normal weather we entered the flat by climbing up two steps to go in the front door. However, after the snow, we opened the front door and climbed up two steps to get out! Snow was so compacted on the roads that motorists, cyclists and pedestrians had to avoid the areas where the manholes were because they looked like harmless puddles but in fact the melted snow over them hid a pit up to three feet deep.

One day during this period, I went to meet Reg from the camp. It started blowing a blizzard, so, being impatient with him for not coming out of the gates on time, I went home soaking wet and in a huff as there was no sign of Reg. Eventually, some two hours later, he came home and I refused to look at him. He didn't and couldn't say much. He had come off his bike on the way to the gates, the bike sliding away from him on the ice as he went around a corner, resulting in his doing a three-point landing and ending up in sickbay where he had some fourteen stitches put into his chin. When I did notice his predicament, all was forgiven as he was lucky not to have received more serious injuries, what with everywhere being a sheet of ice.

Sometimes, one of Reg's friends would visit us, spending the evening in front of the fire doing embroidery. He was doing the work for his fiancée and it was really beautiful: tablecloths, cushion covers and chair backs, all neatly worked in silk. Any woman would have been proud to have accomplished work of such a high standard. I've always admired this kind of work. I asked our landlady if she could recommend a place to buy a baby's shawl, so she wrote to her sister in Lerwick and in due course one arrived. I was able to use it for several of the children that we had. It was handmade and admired by all who saw it.

I loved living in Scotland. The people were so friendly. With the beach just over the road, we could spend hours on the seashore in the summer months. The heather grew very close to the sea and was a picture when in full bloom. One year in the early autumn, we collected a galvanised bucket full of winkles, took them home and cooked them on the kitchen cooker. What a stink! We managed, with the help of the neighbours, to eat the lot, but it took ages to rid the flat of the smell. We also swam and paddled in the sea, it being so clear and clean. Porpoises used to come in really close and play amongst us. They were a bit frightening at first as they could be quite boisterous, bumping into us and knocking us off our feet. When the winter storms came in from the north, huge lobsters were washed ashore where they had been dislodged from a reef about a quarter of a mile out. They were not suitable for eating though, as they'd be battered and broken by the rocks and some were quite old. They could be up to three feet long, from the tip of claw to the end of tail.

At the flat our daughter, who was now toddling and beginning to talk, had a playmate called Sandy. It was great fun, watching them playing and chatting to each other, one with an English accent the other broad Scot. They seemed to understand each other in their own way.

Winter cleared away, and in the fifth month our second daughter was born in Elgin maternity hospital after a few false alarms. I only just made it to the entrance door of the hospital some six miles away before the water broke and she arrived.

Once, on a wet and rainy day, Reg and I were both looking out of the window, trying to make our minds up about a bit of paper across the road at the bus stop. Was it a ten-bob note or not? As it was raining we didn't bother going out just to get soaked over a hunch, so we came away from the window and forgot about it. The next day it was still there and again, not being too sure, we left it alone. The third day – yes! – it was still there, so Reg popped over and picked it up. Ten shillings was a lot in those days, almost like picking up a fiver today, so we were well pleased.

The local fish and chip shops had an unusual item for sale (to us southerners, at least): white pudding sausages. I suppose it was like a haggis, only in the shape of a large deep fried sausage. The other great thing in Scotland were the mutton pies. Reg used to tell the story that while he was working in the blacksmith shop on the camp, he and his mates used to buy one of these pies for the mid-morning snack and put them on the radiator to warm them up. The smell was delicious, but all the gravy and juices used to run down the wall behind the radiator and make a fine mess.

The next posting was to Helston in Cornwall, the opposite end of the country. By now we had got used to moving about the countryside using trains and buses. It was quite an accomplishment to move, the cot on one pedal of my bicycle, with the large case on the other. Two smaller cases were tied to the handlebars and saddle, while the Tansad pram was loaded up with the kids' clothes and food and drink that might be needed on the journey. It was easier than trying to carry all the cases.

The digs in Helston were terrible and I had to give everywhere a thorough cleaning before I could unpack. The property was on top of the hill in the main street of Helston and the water pressure was so low that it took about four or five minutes to fill a kettle. Here I developed a few very large painful boils and suffered a dreadful kidney infection. However, we managed to find alternative digs with the mother of a chief petty officer, a much better situation. After six months we returned to Rustington to live in a house in Jubilee Avenue, sharing with another lodger, a Polish chap who couldn't speak a word of English and his Alsatian dog, Carla. That dog kept pushing her nose into the pram and would insist on licking the baby's face – not at all hygienic! I wasn't very happy with the dog taking so much interest in the child and I kept a wary eye on it, even though I had been given assurances that no harm would come to the baby. Reg was stationed at Anson Site, across the airfield near Yapton. Here he worked on Gannet and Seamew aircraft.

After eight months our next move was to Yeovilton, Somerset. Reg was to pursue a leading airman's course at the Naval Air Station and the family was to live in a hired caravan. This was to be another complete change of thinking for me. How to survive in all weathers and tend to three small children in a home measuring about twenty-two feet long? With an external loo (a bucket) in a tent? There was barely enough room to sit down, let alone turn around. If the wind was blowing... Well, you can imagine what that was like! We had to collect all of our water from a tap alongside another caravan across the road. The road, by the way, was a real country lane, where the cows were driven to be milked, and where the occasional tractor went by. The couple in the caravan opposite proved to be real genuine country folk who would do anything to help anybody – friends and strangers alike. Bob worked on the local farm and Marge was a mine of information, worked for the village church, was a member of St Johns Ambulance and attended all of their local functions, cooking up an all-day breakfast for whoever decided to call. Bob also had a smallholding in the area around his van, but more of that later. We became firm friends, and Marge was more like a mum to me. I loved her dearly and we were destined to meet again later in my story.

At the bottom of the lane was the River Yeo with a weir and stepping stones so that one could cross to get to the field the other side where the footpath led to Lymington village nearly a mile away. There was a pub, The Lamb and Lark, and a house where you knocked on the front door to buy postage stamps and leave your letters for posting. The fields between Yeovilton and Ilchester were so large that they had names, and the one from the stepping stones across the river was called Wellam.

Bob and Marge knew a lady in the cottages near the pub. She often called in to see our friends. She had a Yorkshire accent and when she spoke, after every sentence, she uttered the phrase '…and I was there'.

It wasn't easy with the children in a caravan, but I got used to it. We were only there for four months. A tradesman would come in an old converted green bus, with groceries and paraffin being sold from the baggage compartment at the back. A butcher, fishmonger and a baker called once a week, and a milkman called daily, so we didn't want for anything. There was also the NAAFI shop at the camp. For this I had to cross the main runway. There was a sailor on duty on each side of the runway, and we had to wait for permission to cross. They were always teasing us and on more that one occasion they would say it was OK when an aircraft would come taxiing around the perimeter track and frighten the life out of us, which sent us scurrying, hell for leather across the runway, kids, prams, and shopping in tow.

Myself and the other wives would go to meet our husbands at the end of the day's 'lessons'. For this we had to wait at the main gates of the camp while the classes would come marching down from the aircraft hangars and classrooms. They would cross over the road and assemble in the parade ground opposite the NAAFI. The lads were always led by a drum and bugle band, all marching in unison. Reg was one of the drummers. Being in the band, the members had what was known as a 'Special Duties' card. This enabled the lads to leave the camp and go home every night, if they were living nearby, in exchange for a couple of hour's band practice twice a week. What a laugh! The row that the band made had to be heard to be believed! There was not one drum playing in time with another, and as for the bugles… Well, I reckon that all the players had fat lips and no puff! A cacophony of sound and not a spiritual note amongst them. Harmony and harmonics were nowhere in sight (or sound). The local Sea-cadet Corps were better when they went by on a Remembrance Sunday. Bless their cotton socks, the lads at the camp did try; after all, they were only there for a few months – not really a sufficient time to know one end of a drumstick from the other!

Once a week we would go to Yeovil or Ilchester for shopping. Apart from the noisy aircraft, particularly if they were night flying, life 'down on the farm' wasn't too bad. At weekends, some of the sailors and WRNS would come down to the weir and go skinny-dipping. Marge and I would peer out of our caravan windows with binoculars watching them, not so much as to bring them nearer, but to make every thing look bigger! What a sight! They would have a bonfire and had the equivalent of today's barbecue, complete with beer and snacks. One day, while we were having dinner in the caravan, a hand came through the window holding a can of beer for Reg. When we looked out, there were some of Reg's classmates dressed in nothing more than handkerchiefs across their middle! They had been across to The Lamb and Lark and, on their way back had gone swimming in the river!

Reg's course ended and we went back to Littlehampton, Sussex, where we rented a bungalow. Reg began working at Ford again, across the far side, which was known as Anson site. While there, my third daughter was born. I gave birth to her at my mother's house in Rustington. It was a bad confinement. The child recovered after a traumatic entry into the world, however, with no lasting effects. We had the chance of a council flat in Rustington – our own home at last – but I was disappointed to find that it was an upstairs flat. We had no furniture and very little money so we bought second-hand furniture and mother gave us one or two pieces to help. The people in the downstairs flat were always complaining about our noisy children and one day there was a terrible altercation when both sides came to blows. I continued to write to the council until we got a ground-floor flat. There was something wrong with the chimney in that flat as I was always having chimney fires. They would not come and inspect it so I was always in trouble with the fire brigade.

At that time my husband was away on board HMS Bulwark for ten months with 814 squadron, servicing Seahawks. My health was not good at this time, and the camp personnel and family social advisor put in a request for Reg to fly home. After consultation with Captain Gick, the ship's captain, they decided that Reg should stay where he was, as if he had been flown home on compassionate grounds there was no saying how long he would be home before being shipped off again. When he did come back ten months later, things improved a bit and he was posted back to RNAS Yeovilton. The stories he told us... But that would be another book!

I decided to give up the flat and join him. We bought a caravan and returned to live in a field next to our friends, but on the same side of the road, in Yeovilton village. The children loved it. My son was born in the Maternity Hospital in Yeovilton. After three daughters, at last, I had a son! We all loved him and he was thoroughly spoilt by the girls.

My husband had to go away again on board another aircraft carrier, HMS *Hermes* with 845 squadron, servicing and maintaining helicopters, and just before he sailed off he surprised us all by flying over the caravan in a helicopter and we all waved like mad to each other before he disappeared for a year. The stepping stones had gone and a new road had been built across the fields to Lymington village. I must point out that Yeovilton village had no shops whatsoever. But we now had a bus service with buses on a Tuesday and on a Saturday! There were two buses on each of these days, the first going out and the second in the return direction, so if you missed the first one and caught the return bus to go shopping in the next village you then had the problem of walking home.

This still didn't overcome the annual problem when the River Yeo flooded. Yeovilton village was cut off from the outside world for about two weeks every year when all of the surrounding fields and the road around the side of the airfield was covered in flood water up to a depth of two, sometimes three feet. The locals in the village used to ensure that they kept a stock of tinned food to cover such periods, or rely on milk from the local farm and their own supply of eggs, chickens and produce from their gardens, as it was only the high-wheeled tractors that were able to get through the flood water.

Life went on much the same. Village life with wonderful neighbours is nothing like town life. The door was open to all, and they would just come in. If you weren't there, they'd put the kettle on and wait until you returned. The girls had their own friends in the village, too. At one time Marge was unwell and confined to bed. Her caravan had two doors, one at the kitchen end and the other at the living area end. At night, the latter was turned into the bedroom by pulling down the bed. Friends and neighbours came to visit Marge, and they all turned up at the same time, or so it seemed. They came in one door, stood or sat beside her on the bed chatting away, not only to Marge but also to the people next to them. One moved on and the next in line was already chatting. So it went on and at one time there was a continual queue of people in a circle from one door, through the caravan, out of the other door only to join on the back of the queue that was now in front of them. It would start first thing in the morning until late in the evening. Poor Marge! She was absolutely shattered and was glad of the rest when she felt well enough to get up. Of course the all-day breakfasts were off the menu during this time.

My youngest daughter, Jaycee, formed an attachment to Bob Beaton and loved animals of any kind. There was a pony, a cow, some dogs, chickens and ducks belonging to our friends who lived next door. I especially loved Tansy the Springer Spaniel. Jaycee liked to help Bob milk the cows early in the morning and used to toddle off across the fields with her little red wellies on the wrong feet. She waved a stick that was taller than she was, and went underneath the cows shouting, 'Yoik, yoik, yoik!' to get them moving.

Bob had an old Austin Ruby car and used to take her out in it and she could barely look over the dashboard to see where they were going. At the time, Jaycee was only about four years old and also managed to get rides on the horse and cart. On one occasion, Jaycee came running in, mouth agog and talking so fast that she was spluttering, 'That horse was rude, Mummy!' Evidently Jaycee had been sitting up beside Bob on the cart when the horse had to answer a call of nature, and the horse's backside opened up level with and just in front of Jaycee's face – a sight she had not seen before at such close quarters. The vision offered to her was a big as her little head!

Caravan life was very spartan – all the washing had to be done outside with a cold-water tap and the chemical toilet had to be emptied into a hole in the ground.

One year, Bob and Marge went away for a few days, leaving me in charge to feed the ducks and chickens. When I went to let them out one morning my heart went into my mouth: there were dead ducks all over the orchard, all with their heads bitten off – probably by a fox – and a lonely drake quacking around. There was not a thing I could do but clean up the mess with the help of one of the neighbours.

By then, two other neighbours had joined us in the caravans on either side. We all got on well: Les lived in one, and he was a civilian on the camp working in the electrical department. He only used calor gas for cooking, but the rest of the time his caravan was lit up like Blackpool Tower. He had rigged up a range of batteries charged by a not-too-noisy generating plant. The kids loved him. He was a gentle soul, who had a big bushy white beard and looked a bit like Father Christmas.

On the far side of him were Jean Taylor and Len, more commonly known as 'Buck'. They had a lovely affectionate bulldog called Tich, and he was to be a hero in his own right as will be detailed in the next chapter. Suffice to say that at a crucial time, he managed to drag a heavily pregnant Jean well away from her caravan minutes before the event took place.

The owners of the four caravans obtained permission from the local farmer on whose land we were sited to put in a standpipe connected to Bob and Marge's water line and to put down some paving slabs to make it easier for us all to walk on in the wet weather.

It was a lot of hard work and quite a few drops of sweat hauling the slabs down from the farm and positioning them in a secure and safe manner.

Some years after the next eventful chapter in my life, Bob and Marge finally obtained permission to construct a brick-built bungalow on their piece of land. As a family, we went to visit soon after it was completed, and Reg took some photos of it. When they were processed we noticed on one of the films that the ridge of the bungalow roof was crooked, wavy and undulating. This was sent of to Yeovilton post-haste and we heard later that Bob and Marge had quickly called out the friend responsible for putting on the roof. The day he called to inspect his handiwork it was tipping it down with rain and everyone was soaked. Needless to say they couldn't find anything wrong with the roof – it was the film that had been at fault. It wasn't flat when the picture was printed! Still, it caused a bit of a laugh and a playful thump on the head for Reg when we next visited.

With the building of the bungalow, Bob retired from working on the farm for Roy Wetherall and managed to get a job on the camp as pest control officer (rat-catcher in other words). One day, as he was delivering a welded metal tube that he had strapped to the crossbar of his bike, Prince Charles, who was stationed at the airfield at the time, saw Bob pedalling along with smoke and flames coming out of the end of the tube.

'I say fellow,' he yelled (or something like that), 'your bicycle is on fire!'

While cycling around the camp, the air going down the tube had ignited the rag, which had been tied on before the welding had cooled. Bob stopped and dismounted, looked as the smouldering rag tied on the back, took off his cap, scratched his head, and said in his best Somerset dialect, 'Cor! Bugger I! So it be!'

Due to the Suez Crisis, my husband had to go to the rescue of two tankers that had collided in the Indian Ocean and act as tow ship to take one of them up to the Persian Gulf to safety. For this reason he was away longer than expected –ten months in fact. On the ship they had a radio programme that was broadcast to the ship's company. It was made up of requests from the wives and sweethearts for favourite songs and messages. During the delay, the captain of the ship had one of his own as a personal message to the ship's company. It was, 'I know where I'm going, and I know who's going with me!' Well, they couldn't do much else, could they?

Reg eventually went to Portsmouth, and was discharged in 1961 from the navy having completed ten years' service. While on demob leave we made plans for the future. He got a job on the local navy air station with a civilian aircraft company, Airworks Services, (they were allowed to start work in civilian street before their actual leaving date), servicing the same type of aircraft that he was familiar with but with about one-third less pay. Before he started his job he suggested I spend a week in Surrey with his parents, as I needed a break. I agreed to go as long as he promised to look after the children properly. I had some reservations about leaving them, as Steven was only about six months old. I went first to Surrey where Reg's parents had a prefab. During the week my mother-in-law took me to London to meet all her relatives. I walked miles around London, my legs aching and my feet hurting as I didn't have a decent pair of shoes. She took me up and down the underground, and half the time I did not know one relative from another, as there seemed to be no end to them and I was never quite sure to whom I was talking. Consequently, I was glad to go back to my family for a rest although I did appreciate the hospitality from my in-laws. My husband then returned to work at the airfield with Airworks to work on the planes that were to act as targets for the naval pilots when they went on aerial manoeuvres. As it happened, he was with them for only a month.

The story now moves on to the next phase of my life.

2

A Near-Death Experience

I had been having a recurring dream at night. There was a tall building made of glass in the dream. I could see the sun reflecting on the glass and flames and smoke coming up from the ground like great clouds. I could not make sense of this dream at all. I had this same dream over several weeks, and I told my husband that it may be a premonition of some kind. I thought he might be in danger working on the airfield. On one summer day in July the day began as any other. The children were ready for school; my husband went off to work and I walked the children to school up the lane.

Having returned, Jaycee played in the field adjacent to the caravan. I put my little boy down in his pram for a nap while I got on with the housework and at about 9.20 that morning my daughter called to me to come outside. I refused and got on with the washing up. She called me and I ignored her for the second time. I wish I had gone outside after what happened next, but it is useless to have regrets. There was a horrible roaring sound: my caravan had been torn apart by an aircraft. I saw a plane with a pilot in the cockpit come past my kitchen window between the two caravans, the pilot's eyes looking at me through his face mask and goggles. I was shocked to see him even though it was only for a few seconds. Time and motion then stood still, before he whooshed forward and the wing of the plane sliced through the caravan. It came through from behind me carrying the coal fire with it. This in turn hit the back of my legs, crushing me against the cooker and the sink before carrying on to crash through the hedge and across a neighbour's garden, ending up lodged in the wall next to the French windows of a lovely old ham stone house that had solid eighteen-inch-thick stone walls. Unfortunately, the pilot was killed on impact. I let go of the sink where I had been holding myself up and fell to the floor. I then pulled myself along the floor by my elbows towards a hole in front of me at the end of the caravan. I threw myself out onto the grass in a head-down attitude; the roof collapsed completely and lay across my thighs, which somehow stopped all of my blood draining away. My head and shoulders were on the ground and what was left of my legs still in the caravan.

I was in complete shock, not realising the extent of my injuries, but I did not lose consciousness completely. I lay there for some time and I was partially aware of some people coming and staring at me. After what seemed an age the sailors of the crash crew came and took me to hospital on a stretcher in an ambulance.

I saw my daughter Jaycee standing by the gate crying as I was lifted into the ambulance. She said, 'You are going to die, Mummy' and I replied, 'Don't cry, I'll be back'. I wished so much at the time that I could have gone to her and comforted her, but I felt so tired and could not move on the stretcher.

When I got to the hospital the stretcher was too long to go into the lift and I had to be manhandled with the stretcher and carried up the stairs. In the room next to the operating theatre I was X-rayed, cleaned up and about this time Reg had arrived and with the nurses trying to get me undressed. Reg took charge, and taking a pair of scissors off one of the nurses cut my clothes off, bottom to top. After all, it was the quickest way without subjecting me to extra pain and distress in the damaged state that I was in. I was then rushed into surgery and remember having an injection to put me to sleep. At that point I dreamed I was passing through the air and travelling along a tunnel, rolling like a ball at great speed. Near the end of the tunnel was a very bright light. I could hear voices singing, like a choir. The music was beautiful and I could see a lovely rainbow. When I reached the bright, shining light I stopped as the light filled the tunnel. Then a voice spoke to me. It was as if the light itself was saying 'It is not your time to go yet – you must go back.' I had no knowledge of returning to my body but felt myself being shaken and told to wake up. I was back with the living, but I had very nearly died and felt more than a little ashamed at not wanting to come back. The surgeon came to see me and told me my right leg had been amputated through the knee and the left leg above the knee. I had also been given copious amounts of blood. He said I would walk again one day but at the time I doubted him. However, he was right and eventually I did. Reg told me afterwards that he had managed to get to the hospital before I was taken to surgery and said that I was drifting in and out of consciousness, able to say a few words. He told me that I still had a Polo mint in my mouth from before the plane had hit! The only other mark I had was a small scratch about half an inch long on my temple.

Some years after the accident, Reg was able to obtain a cassette called 'Inward Harmony'. There was a leaflet with the cassette that told of a man who had visited a music fayre, picked up a pair of earphones that had some music playing through them, had gone white and took off the earphones and walked away. Some time later he returned, listened to the music again and spoke to the stallholder. It turned out that the stallholder, while meditating one day, heard the music and wrote the score while in trance. The man then said that the music that was on the cassette was identical to that which he had heard while having a near death experience.

The accident happened at 9.20 a.m. on Tuesday 21 July 1961, two days before a horrific murder on the A27 and the Valerie Storey incident in the headlines of the general press succeeded each other. Reg said afterwards that when he went back to the site the same day to salvage what could be rescued he found the field where the wreckage was filled with ghouls, souvenir hunters they called themselves, picking up anything that they could: small ornaments, some of the souvenirs that Reg had brought back from abroad and even some of the children's toys and clothing that they thought might come in handy. The village policeman stood there helpless with tears running down his face. Reg managed to send some of them packing but not all. People always accumulate at disaster zones, and it will always be so, until humanity learns to respect other people's feelings and possessions.

I spent the first few weeks of my convalescence in Yeovil General Hospital. I was relying on strong medication for the pain and I could not lie down on my ripple bed which was supplied to prevent bedsores forming. I had to sleep sitting up so I spent a lot of time cat napping day and night, unable to have a full night's rest. My husband spent most days at my bedside in a state of shock at the situation we had found ourselves in. I had a very good physiotherapist who gave me a strong wooden board (which we called Fred) to enable me to slide from bed to wheelchair and back again. Once I started moving about it was a great help to me and I was given exercises each day so I would not get too immobile.

I had difficulty coming to terms with the situation. I missed my children a great deal and hoped that they were being taken care of. I did not want them to go into a home but felt it might be inevitable. Reg had had several offers via the camp commander but he arranged for them to stop with my mother and father-in-law. However, they were not able to cope because of their age and had got out of the way of caring for children. After a month they took them to my own mother in Sussex. Mum and my stepdad had agreed to take them in. It was a lot to ask of anyone – four additional children were a lot of extra work.

I had a visit from a lieutenant commander from the air station in all his gold braid and carrying his ceremonial sword. He asked me if there was anything I would like to raise my spirits, and I said I would love some fresh flowers in my room. From then on I had a bouquet every week. This cheered me up no end and the staff were very kind to me.

Before I left Yeovil I also received another lovely bouquet of flowers from the pilot's widow. It was such a kind gesture as she had lost a husband and father to her three children. It must have been devastating for her, and I often wondered how she felt about the tragedy and how it would have affected her life. Soon after the accident Reg moved to Farnham in Surrey to live with his parents and got himself a job with an engineering firm in Aldershot.

Convalescence

Reg had to make some decisions. He could not work on the airfield again due to the association of accident and planes and had to find alternative work. With the caravan destroyed, Reg moved into lodgings in Yeovil. Sid Carter, who he was staying with, was a driving instructor with the army and he taught Reg to drive in a Ford Prefect 100E side valve, which he bought two days after the accident, knowing that I would have to be mobile. I learnt afterwards that while out on the road Sid had tied a piece of string to each of Reg's ankles and, holding onto the other end of the string, would pull on a string and stamp on one of Reg's feet to ensure that he had pressed or disengaged the right pedal in the correct sequence and at the right time! Reg passed his test first time, on market day in a snowstorm and with an iced-up windscreen!

Reg was able to take me out after I had been moved to South Petherton for further convalescence. The place was full of elderly people and I made friends with a woman in a wheelchair called Eve who suffered from diabetes and had had a leg removed, and also with the porter and his wife. But I found the place very depressing and only saw Reg about once a month. I was taken out occasionally in the car with Dave the porter and we were invited to their home to meet the family and then I was transferred to Frenchay Hospital to learn to walk on little short legs called pylons. These were like artificial legs but were made with the feet facing backwards and were placed where my knees would have been. The man who taught me to walk with these pylons prepared me for when I would have to go to Roehampton and walk on full-sized limbs.

While in Somerset, my stepfather bought my family to see me in his Reliant three-wheeler van – green, not yellow like Del Boy's. It must have been a long journey for them, cooped up in the little van, but he did it more than once in order to keep my morale up and to give me the chance to see my children. I will always be grateful to him for all that he did for my family. There will always be a special place in my heart for him.

I was informed that I was now going to be transferred to Roehampton for six weeks or so, so that I could be fitted with full-size artificial limbs and learn to walk properly. It was hard trying to regain my balance as the limbs were pointing down to the floor while my phantom limbs were sticking straight out in front of me. Also, the ends of my stumps hadn't fully healed yet. At times it felt as if it was going to be an impossible task, but my incentive was to get home again and be with my family. I often thought of Our Lord in those days and how much He suffered on the cross before He died.

Pain in the phantom limb is still occasionally a problem to this day, the worst times being when it feels as if a dog is gnawing one of the bones that aren't there, or as if my foot is being screwed off at the ankle!

A New Life

Meanwhile, Reg had written to our local MP, who raised a question in the House. We were given an advance on the compensation that would eventually come our way and Reg was able to arrange the purchase of a new bungalow in Thorne Road, in the Shortheath/Boundstone area near Rowledge, Farnham.

We went shopping for the furniture in Guildford, at Courts. We bought everything: beds, dressing tables, wardrobes, a sideboard, a dining table and chairs and a coffee table. The whole lot cost us, in those days, just under £300! We also had to buy new clothes for the kids and ourselves as all had been lost or damaged in the accident, not so much burnt as contaminated with the fibreglass insulation from the walls of the caravan. Nothing could really be salvaged. It was a tremendous shopping list, and after making the selection of all that was required, Reg realised that he didn't have the chequebook. Panic set in, but all turned out well as the shop manager had a blank chequebook for such an occasion. I can't see shopkeepers being so forgiving these days!

With everything installed we went down to Sussex to collect the family. It was an exciting time, as I hadn't seen them that often during my convalescence and general rehabilitation. The accident was in the July of the previous year and now it was March 1962. It was going to be difficult for the children, as they had their own school friends and other people that they had grown to know well. However, I wasn't prepared for what my mother now said to me. She wanted to keep our son and bring him up as her own! He was two years and ten months old and had become accustomed to my mother and stepfather – there did seem to be a bond between them. But I could not agree to part with my only son under any circumstances. I refused and we were able to relocate as planned in Farnham. My mother pleaded with me to let her keep him for a little longer, but I had to have him back so that I could get to know him again. I loved him and the girls and this is what I had survived and struggled for.

We settled in and the girls were found a place at the local village school in Rowledge. I was confined to the house with our little son who was not responding to or accepting me. I contacted social services for assistance and asked if they could find a playschool for him so that he could benefit from interacting with other children of his own age. A place was found for him but all he did was cry all the time. It was heartbreaking and they said it wasn't doing him any good, so he had to stay at home with me. He responded to his sisters and his father but still not to me. I was upset and hurt by this and wondered if it would have been the right thing to let him stop with my mother. Reg assured me that, given time, he would eventually come round.

We decided to change the car from our trusty Ford Prefect, and bought a new Vauxhall Cresta, a luxury car for us, with a front bench seat and column change gearbox. This was fine except that the gear control would fall apart and leave us in first gear at the most inconvenient times, usually at the traffic lights by the Bush Hotel in Farnham. This would result in a slow-crawl tailback until the road widened and traffic could pass. Reg, bless his cotton socks, managed to fix the short screw that kept coming loose so that it wouldn't keep getting us into trouble.

I gradually learnt to adapt to the limbs and could manage some of the household chores. At first I sat on the floor to do what I could at that level and then put the limbs on to do the higher things standing up. I still found it difficult and the end of the stumps was painful and not healing very well. I was shut in and couldn't make friends. Our bungalow was one of five with three houses adjacent in a cul-de-sac. I invited some of the neighbours around for tea, coffee and biscuits, but they were ill-at-ease with me, and not once did I receive an invite round to their houses although I could see them visiting each other through our windows. Some people are very unkind and do not realise how much a rebuff like this can hurt. I did manage to make friends with an older woman across the way, who came in and helped me with some of the housework. We became firm friends and I used to go to her place for a cuppa.

My mother-in-law noticed that I wasn't adapting to my new legs very well and decided (without consulting me) to talk to her doctor about the problem. He came to the bungalow unexpectedly and told me in no uncertain terms to pull myself together and stop worrying my husband and family. I was very upset, I can tell you; I wasn't this doctor's patient, so why was he bothering to come and see me? It didn't help me being spoken to in that tone of voice, but I decided that I *would* pull myself together and show them that I really was made of sterner stuff! I did build up confidence, and went on improving my outlook. At that time there wasn't the facility of counselling to overcome accident trauma; one just had to pick up the pieces and get on with life. I guess our perspective on life was different in those days.

Life continued and we had an extension built onto the bungalow, giving us a further bedroom. While here, we experienced another hard winter, and our electricity bill for the cold period was over £100 for the quarter. It turned out that there was a fault with the under-floor electric heating, but we didn't find out until after we moved some three years later.

While there, we decided to change our car so that I could learn to drive and we looked round for a small automatic car that could be converted to hand controls. We finally saw a DAF belt-driven car. They had just become available on the English market as they originated from Holland. Each winter after that Mother insisted that we were to accept the can of anti-freeze that she bought us. This was a total waste of time as the DAF had an air-cooled engine and didn't require anti-freeze, but she wouldn't have that as an excuse!

Another Move

Next, back to Rustington. Another bungalow, but along the road from where Mother lived. It had three bedrooms, a lounge and separate dining room. There was a willow tree about five foot from one of the bedrooms so that had to be cut down to prevent damp and to give more light into the room. Along the front of the bungalow bamboos had been planted which were over six-foot high, but the roots were beginning to undermine the footings so they had to come out too.

Reg found a job with a company that manufactured photo-copying machines just down the road, practically opposite. Steven was about to start primary school and I found a place for him a few yards down the road. This was handy as the three girls could take him for me and keep an eye open for his safety and bring him home.

I also started to take driving lessons. After a few lessons I was successful in passing my driving test. Freedom at last! When I got back to the bungalow and reversed into the drive, I hit the pillar of the gatepost. The car had a nasty dent, and it didn't do the gatepost much good either! Not a very good start. I took a lot more care after that and became more confident. I was able to take the children to school and take my mother out to do some shopping and drive to the hairdressers. I was a lot more inde-pendent. I was able to walk about the garden and do limited weeding and plant flowers while sitting on a mat on the ground. My dad came to visit me with his second wife and son who was three years old and suffered from spina bifida. He was a lovely, fair-haired little boy named Peter. They only visited me once but it was great to see my dad again after all those years.

The girls were getting older changing schools and went the secondary school. They always had a lot of friends in the house and it was a happy home for a while. Then, as they approached puberty and their teen years, things became different. Arguments and bad behaviour became the norm. I found it difficult to keep the peace between them, and my husband would lose his temper and shout at them. I did my best to reason with them but things went from bad to worse and they would stay out all night and drink too much. They told lies and played truant and the eldest got so drunk at times that my husband had to collect her from the pub because she had passed out.

They started smoking and going out with boys and as I felt it was normal I encouraged them to bring their boyfriends home. I was not getting any help with the chores, only excuses, so I let them go out, remembering my own childhood when I did not have any free time. But it got to the point where I could not cope any more and so I called in the social worker to give me advice as to what to do with them. One of them was over sixteen and I was told that I could not do much about her. She took an overdose and had to go to hospital. This again caused a great deal of upset in the family. I look back on all the temper tantrums, the rows and broken crockery, but we got through it and braced ourselves for what might come next. Our youngest daughter, Jaycee, was going out with a boy who would climb through her bedroom window at night. One evening, my husband caught him and this caused more rows and upsets, though I could not do anything about it. However, she did eventually marry this man.

I had had a miscarriage myself two years prior to this and being a double-leg amputee I was told that I would not able to carry a child full-term anymore. I went into the local maternity hospital for a sterilisation operation and afterwards felt depressed for some time as they thoughtlessly put me in a ward with mums who had just had their babies.

The girls took an interest in an Ouija board they had borrowed from a friend. I did not like them having it in the house but they persisted with it, not knowing what they were doing. Reg tried to dissuade them by running his finger round the rim of a glass goblet to make it hum and tried hanging strings of buttons outside the window of their room so they'd make tapping noises on a windless night, but to no avail. Things began to happen and I started being woken by a young girl in the night. I knew she was an earthbound spirit; she would beckon me to follow her through the door and down the hallway where she would fade as she passed through the lounge wall. This happened several times.

My husband lost his job and was out of work for several months. Ella wanted to marry and leave us but I felt she should wait until she was older. This caused more rows, upsets and days of bad tempers and so I gave in and let her marry; she wore me down. Reg was very unhappy about it all and I was left to make the wedding arrangements myself. About the same time my mother had asked me for a loan a buy a bungalow and, against my husband's advice, I loaned her the money. My stepfather had an agreement drawn up to pay the money back and unfortunately he died of cancer of the pancreas before the debt was fully paid. After the funeral, my mother, in anger and grief, said that he had killed himself by working too hard to pay off the debt. In fact, after working on oil tankers for all of his life before retiring from the merchant navy, the real cause was more probably due to being in the presence of crude oil fumes, coupled with being a habitual heavy smoker. It is no good saying 'if only I had known' and that I wouldn't have loaned him the money if I had; we can all be wise after the event. Poor Bow was a good man, one of the best. I wish he had not had to suffer so much and I will always remember him for his patience and understanding in difficult times and the way he cared for my children while I was in hospital. I think of him a lot and know he is watching over us and Mother in spirit.

Reg had applied for a job in Lancing and we were overjoyed to hear he had secured the position. We decided to sell the bungalow and move closer to his new work place, halving the travelling distance. We went house-hunting and found what we were looking for. Our bungalow was sold and our new home ready to move into. On our moving day I asked Jaycee to move in with us and our son and she said she would rather go to live with her boyfriend in a bedsit. Ella was living in a flat with her husband and baby son and was now expecting another child. My husband was working at a medical equipment company – he was in charge of the twilight shift, from five in the evening until one in the morning, with 134 female workers who finished at eleven, making hospital equipment.

With the bungalow we had to start from scratch, redecorating throughout and cultivating the garden. There was a lot to do with the spare time that we had as all that Reg missed was the television programmes, and still got a reasonable night's sleep, as well as getting to know the neighbours. However, one side was somewhat difficult to get on with. After a while, having made our feelings clear, we settled for an existence with neither neighbour trusting nor speaking to the other. When the family came to visit and children played in the garden, if a ball went over the fence they would not give it back and if the children went round to ask for it that was deemed wrong too. In the end we bought a swing ball on a rope to stop the rows, and life went on.

Ella's second child, a daughter, was born with breathing problems. Her heart would stop and we'd have to call the ambulance for help. She had trouble eating and was not able to swallow properly and kept regurgitating her food. I asked the doctor to call in a paediatrician who got her into a hospital for some tests. Within two days she was transferred to Great Ormond Street children's hospital and it turned out that Joanne had too much fatty tissue around all the muscles in her body as well as heart problems. She had to be fed by tube and spent the first year of her life in hospital. In spite of being hyperactive and having physical mobility problems, she has since grown up and had two healthy boys, bringing them up as a single mum. I will never forget going to visit her in hospital in London during the IRA bombings, which was a scary time, but we got through it.

As Joanne grew older and really before she started school, she started talking about the Amish that she used to live with. This was a pre-life experience, and at the time we had no idea who they were. She used to talk about the way they dressed, how the men and women were segregated and how all work was for the good of the community. What we couldn't establish however was, were they from Germany where the Amish originated, or were they one of the American sects?

Our eldest was living in Wick and we heard that she and her husband had parted. Again we heard nothing from her for a year or two and then she suddenly phoned and asked if she could come home. She stayed for a few weeks, was not in a very good state of health and had hit the drugs scene. She then went steady with another chap and said she was leaving to take a job in Wales with him. She left the following morning and again it was another two years before we heard she was living in East Preston with the boyfriend who she had married when her first son was born. A daughter and another son then followed. Gary left her and she had to take in a lodger to help pay the bills. She worked in pubs amongst other things. A minder looked after her children and once they had started school she was able to work longer hours.

She loved to spend her evenings in the pub and always ended up the worse for drink. The children generally looked after themselves and I felt sorry for them but there was little I could do except have them over and give them some good food. They were always hungry.

Finally, the drink having got the better of her, she fell down a staircase and banged her head on the concrete floor. She was taken to Worthing Hospital in a coma and transferred to Haywards Heath where she remained in a coma for a further seven days. When she finally came round she did not know her family, anyone or anything. The consultant had said that her brain was like a jelly in a biscuit tin that had been thrown against the wall and there was no saying what the future would bring. Only time would tell if she would respond to rehabilitation. Her boyfriend took her home before we could make the rehabilitation arrangements but she should never have gone home as she was – it was far too soon. He and social services ensured that we did not see her again. He came to the house and gave my husband a beating, then turned on me, nearly knocking me out of my wheelchair. We refused to accept the blame for what had happened to her – she had chosen her own path and he wasn't any good for her as he encouraged the drinking instead of trying to help her get off the scourge.

Jaycee lived in Littlehampton with her husband when her first daughter was born. After some time they found that they were not compatible after all and he left, leaving a note on the mantelpiece! She then met someone else and had another daughter but that relationship soon ended. She moved to Washington at that time and there she met Dave and moved to Kent where she had a son, but that marriage did not last long either! It was here that she met Nigel and came back to Sussex to live in Worthing; they been happily married for several years. The children are now all adults, have children of their own and are in regular contact with both their mum and their own fathers.

While at Rustington and soon after I had passed my driving test, I managed to get a part-time job in a local factory that made demonstration and teaching aids for medical schools and colleges. Most of the time I hand-painted in fine detail the various body parts that had been bought in, such as models of eye diseases, cross-section models of knee, ankle and hand joints, etc. It was very interesting work and I enjoyed being able to do something useful. One day, I was working with a male colleague and we didn't speak to each other all day due to mutual embarrassment. A batch of male body parts had arrived and we had to paint them in fine detail in all sorts of colours depending on the race that they represented: black, brown, white... You name it, we had to do it! Normally I am partial to chocolate éclairs and Reg had bought some for our tea when I got home that day, but somehow I couldn't really face them!

While all this was going on my artificial legs were wearing out and needed some urgent repairs. A visit to the Brighton Rehabilitation Centre was necessary, and I had an assessment from a very nice man, Brian. Due to the condition of my pins he recommended that I should be fitted with an up-to-date new pair. Several attempts were made, and more than a few different types were tried: suction ones that didn't need a belt and one particular type that had a pin in the end which I needed Reg's help to locate, as the pin sat in a concealed hole in the bottom of the socket on the lower part of the limb. On one occasion, when we got home and I wanted to take the legs off, I couldn't unlock the lower bit from the leg socket – they had forgotten to refit the release pin! Reg, with his trusty toolbox, had to find a way to do it. This resulted in another trip to Brighton. This design would probably have been all right, however, if my smaller stump was another two or three inches shorter, as the assembled prosthesis, due to its design, ended up with one knee at a lower level than the other one. However, I wasn't going to put myself through more pain and anguish by having a further operation!

On another occasion I had a fitting and had arranged to have the limbs sent directly home instead of going to Brighton yet again. You wouldn't believe it! When they arrived one of the legs had the knee joint fixing some four inches higher than the other! Yet another time the limbs were brought to me out of the workshop with two left feet! They laughed thinking it very funny, but believe you me, I just blew my top! After some ten years of trial and error, they had to copy the design of my original pair, and even these I tend to keep as spares, while I continue wearing the first ones issued some forty-five years ago, though the leather's a bit cracked and they creak. In all that time they have never been able to match the colour of the feet with the colour of the shins, so I have to wear short knee-highs under my long full-length stockings. Brian created none of the above problems, bless his cotton socks. He did the best he could and was very apologetic; the faults lay with the manufacturing departments.

Our son Steven grew up to be a hard worker. His first job was making rocking horses in Arundel and it was here that he got the feel of working with wood. He worked for Bentalls for a while, laying carpets and fitting curtains and there he met a man who promised to teach him upholstery. He worked with him and learned the trade and then worked for two other local companies to expand his experience. With a girlfriend and some money from the sale of a flat, he was able to start his own business. He now has a shop in Petworth and a workshop in Halnaker near Chichester. He sells carpets, curtains and furniture and in the workshop has three men working a full week doing upholstery. I am really proud of him and he has since married and has two adopted children who are doing well with their education, one at college and one at university.

While at the bungalow in Durrington, I had a nervous breakdown, and as part of the recovery programme I was successful in getting a place at a day centre where we had social interaction with others that were not so physically capable. The instructors here were a dream! I soon overcame my psychological problems and my life rapidly returned to 'normal'. I also managed to attend the one at Rustington and between them both I learnt many new skills. The day at these centres started at nine in the morning until four in the afternoon with a decently cooked lunch thrown in – all for about £2.50 per day. It got me out of the house and I was able to interact socially with other people.

The new skills involved leatherwork, shaping and engraving the leather, making belts carved with oak and pine leaves and other patterns and handbags. All were difficult, as one couldn't make a mistake without spoiling the finished article. These also had to be dyed to enhance the flower and leaf patterns. The one that I was able to keep is so good that I'm afraid to take it out in case it gets pinched!

Among the smaller items we made were bookmarks. Plaster-work was also a must for the nativity sets that had to be made for the Christmas sales and chess sets in various styles as well as wall plaques and christening plates with names on. We produced plaster-stone clocks with different scenes and figures moulded onto them and fitted the timepieces and hanging loops. Christmas time also meant that production had to go ahead for plastic canvas work in the shape of angels and other Christmas tree decorations. We made advent calendars, sewed patchwork, including a group of us doing a patchwork bedspread. We crocheted rugs and made tapestry pictures, several of which I managed to sell but managed to keep several more. There were also cross-stitch samplers, tapestry cushions, pressed flowers for greetings cards and a process using a liquid plastic to dip flower-shaped arrangements to make transparent flowers and leaves. These were really effective and I haven't seen anything like them outside of the day centres. I had the opportunity to use a small model maker's lathe, turning small pieces of wood to make rails and bedposts for dolls' furniture. Mosaic work was also on the curriculum, as were patterned trays and plaques using stone chippings or dried seeds, beans and pulses and beads. Peg bags and aprons were also on the list, so you can see we were kept quite busy throughout the year.

At the Rustington centre, a different regime was in place, with a different set of instructors. However, here I learnt to paint with new materials such as oils, acrylic and water paints. Silk painting and tie n' dip processes were learnt. Here they had a fully-fledged pottery room with a proper kiln, so more could be dabbled with. We had expert tuition so fewer accidents happened with the pottery pieces collapsing, and the discipline in this room was very strict so nobody burnt themselves on the kiln. Again I was able to sell some of my paintings.

In all I was at the day centres for about ten years until one closed and the other became too far to get to as the funding for the bus put it outside of the catchment area. I had a lot of fun learning the skills, as well as the occasional run out on the bus with the centre to local pubs for lunch. We didn't work on these afternoons... I wonder why?

We were experiencing problems at Durrington with the local yobs who were damaging residents' property and generally being more than a nuisance, and so we decided to move into a sheltered, warden-assisted flat. Here we had a noisy neighbour who gave the residents no peace and he actually broke windows of the residents' flats, lit fires and broke down trees on the premises. The housing association took him to court and, although they won the case, the problem was not resolved until three years later when the troublemaker gained financially after being ordered by the court to dispose of his property. This didn't particularly worry him as he was actually living in another property in Lancing at the time of the disturbances.

With the worry of the court case, where we were called as witnesses, we decided to move again and bought another flat, again warden-assisted, just off the seafront in Worthing. Being on the second floor, we experienced more ups and downs, but one in particular caused great amusement to the wardens and other residents. One day, when we returned from a shopping trip, we found that the lift was out of order. Anita, the duty warden, promptly phoned the fire brigade. First to arrive was the fire officer to assess the situation. Having determined that some big fellows were required, he called the duty fire crew. It not being a real priority call they took a little time arriving but once there, without any further ado, they bodily lifted me, still in my wheelchair, and carried me up two storeys which necessitated negotiating four flights of stairs! On this occasion it was not too long before the lift engineer arrived and corrected the fault. More recently, though, a failure of the electrics resulted in the lift being out of action for twelve days, as spare parts are no longer manufactured and the service company had to locate a replacement part that one of their engineers in Scotland had in his van. Talk about solitary confinement!

3

Finding New Beginnings

Over the years in the past, we had toyed with the notion that we needed to attend a church, and eventually, in June 2003 (we had moved that February) we decided to go to the spiritualist church in Grafton Road, Worthing. We chose a Sunday evening service as it would be quiet and would give us a taster of how the service was conducted. The service started in the usual way with prayers and hymns. A medium was introduced, who started to give clairvoyant readings. We did not know demonstrations of clairvoyance were part of the service and were most surprised when the medium came to me and described my Aunty Dolly. It was said that she loved flowers and that she was one of my guardians in Spirit. On the other side in Spirit, she has a cottage and tends to her flower garden including the tall delphiniums (which were her favourite flowers when on the earth plane). Another aunt was then described who loved to play cards for pennies with other members of the family and a cousin brought forward as well. Following that, a very dear friend from Somerset was described, but this will be discussed in detail later on.

We did not know anyone in the church and they did not know us. The medium was from up north, so there was no way that he could possibly have known any of our relatives or friends. I came away from that service really elated. I loved the peace in the church and knew that I had chosen the right one. In fact, we became hooked, as it were, and became regular attendees at the church. When we got back home that evening I phoned my son Steven and told him all about the experiences we had just had. While talking to him on the phone, my aunt's head and shoulders appeared on the wall of the lounge as if she was alive. It was an incredible feeling, I can tell you. We bought a hardback notebook and started to record this reading and most of the others that we started to receive. It changed our lives. We asked the church president if there was a circle that we could join, and eventually we were introduced to Meg and her husband, Neris, an unusual name but one he was given as he was born during the sounding of an air-raid siren and it was this word spelt backwards. We were invited to join their group in the hall at the back of Grafton Road church. We attended this for several weeks and learnt what went on and how messages came from the other side. Meg invited us to go for healing at Mill Road where she and Neris were the senior healers. It was here that we met GH and in the following February we joined her weekly awareness circle and further advanced our capabilities with psychometry, angel card readings, working with colour and ribbons and learnt the rudiments of meditation and how one should protect oneself. Both events continued for some months and we asked Meg if we could be taught how to become healers ourselves. She was glad to take us under her wing and we duly became adept at giving healing. The following year, Meg and Neris resigned from the healing group, which was governed by The National Spiritualist Union. The healing group would now have had to close its doors, but we were immediately able to keep going under the new name of the Worthing Spiritual Healers, and have been successful in keeping the doors open ever since.

Our awareness opened up when we met Helen in the flat below us and had weekly sessions with her on Spiritual matters, both hands-on experience and philosophy. Also, two healers came to give healing once a fortnight, so we continued receiving healing there until the time came when the man was diagnosed with cancer and they had to stop work. We had meetings in our flat, read Spiritualist books and slowly began to unfold spiritually. I've often been told of the benefit that people have received after a session of healing. Reg often helped people at work who had stiff shoulders or were unwell and I always knew he would be doing God's work because I had seen him help so many people. One day, we were at a meeting with Helen when she asked me to place my hands in hers. I did so and was filled with something like a power surge which went right through me. I had received tremendous power from the Spirit world through my friend, which enabled me to become a healer. We joined awareness and development circles at the Mill Road SNU church and stayed in those circles for some eighteen months.

Circle Meditations

Some of the experiences that I had while meditating in the circles were new to me, and it should be remembered that you, reader, may not necessarily experience the same things as me. Everyone is different, coming from different backgrounds and creeds and everyone has different thoughts on spirituality. Again, I would reiterate that the visions that come into the mind are not imagination or brought to the mind by you directing the images to appear. These images are like those on a TV screen, where you do not know what is coming next. A guided meditation instructs or suggests a starting point, an image to start you on a journey perhaps, but then you are left to your own devices and other new images start to appear. Sometimes a person will receive nothing at all, and another may only get symbols. Two suggested guided meditations are at the end of this section.

Some of the images are what legends and stories of old are made of. You may not only see people and places, but also animals of all kinds including legendary animals such as the unicorn or Pegasus. Elementals may also appear. These are the guardians of nature such as elves, fairies, leprechauns and the divas of trees.

Below are a few meditations from the scores that we have had, to give you some idea of what you might expect when you start in your own circle.

5 February 2005

This was our first awareness circle, presided over by GH whom we had met the previous November when we attended the first healing session, as suggested by Meg.

As is the norm, the evening was opened with a prayer of thanks for bringing us together, and a prayer for protection against those energies which may not be conducive to a safe gathering, and introduced ourselves by name so that we knew who was who. All such introductory rituals are important and should be adhered to at all meetings. There were fourteen people at this first meeting.

GH gave us a partial guidance introduction, leading me to be aware of a window with a vase and a flower in it. I saw a dark red rose in bud and the vase was on a windowsill. It opened into a full-blown rose with yellow stamens in the centre. The perfume filled my head and invaded my senses. I turned my head towards the window, saw a scene that I have never seen before, and I was suddenly standing on a beach on the seashore. A man in a brown mackintosh approached me and sat on a seat close to me. He had a newspaper under his arm and was holding a walking stick. Nothing was said. Then my gran came into the picture and I was aware of two dogs playing on the beach. They were my old friends Boysee and Jilly, my stepfather's long-haired Old English sheepdog. She was one of the small varieties and loved chasing rats and rabbits. A small girl and a boy were playing in the sand and then I was aware of my stepfather, Bow, smiling at me. He threw a stick for the dogs to fetch.

Doff (my mother's sister) came to say hello, then GH called us back to our normal time/space in the here and now: we came to and opened our eyes. GH then asked each of us in turn to relate what we had seen in meditation and some astounding facts were shared.

We were then split into groups of three and had healing instruction with two giving and one receiving. AG, a Scots lady with some years experience, was able to pick up details of my accident and my out-of-body experience at the time. She also picked up a nun in a blue habit who was always around me. AG identified my mother with all her characteristics and wasn't far out with her age. She also said that there was a lot of cold around her, which I understood. I was told that I should wear more bright colours; I tended at the time to wear a lot of navy blue and black. The following day I went shopping and bought a light coloured cardigan and a light blue blouse.

We changed positions, with AG receiving, and I picked up a lot of tension around her. She acknowledged the fact that she was worried about her sister who was ill in hospital, and about other family matters.

GH then closed the circle with a prayer for closure and protection on our journey home. The evening then ended with informal chat, tea and biscuits.

I felt that we had made the right decision and that we were now going in the right direction. We felt comfortable and among like-minded people. It is important that if you are not sure how to make contact with like-minded people you should in the first instance try to establish where your nearest spiritualist church might be and start attending on a regular basis. As you get to know the other members you can then make enquiries about the circles that are held. Several crystal shops also hold meditation circles, but be aware, some work with the earth energies and are not necessarily spiritual.

10 February 2005

This was a short meditation, and all I saw was a black and white dog. From the description and characteristics I gave, it turned out to be Reg's dog, Whiskey, sometimes known to the family as Buster. This dog evidently was a real character and had as a friend, a mouse that came up through the hole in the floorboards under the sink where the drain pipes were. Reg's dad used to encourage the mouse into the living room by feeding it chocolate and cheese. One day, Whiskey chased the mouse back down the hole, sticking his nose in and sniffing for the mouse when it turned and bit him on the nose. The dog sat back with a surprised look on his face. After that the two animals used to sit side by side in front of the fire, or so I'm told, anyway!

14 February 2005

Having meditated and while receiving healing, I had a vision of Reg and I in a field full of grass and wild flowers beside a large lake. As we walked to the water's edge I saw a sailing boat with my mother seated in it. I asked Reg to get in to stabilise the boat to prevent it tipping over. When I looked back to the boat my stepfather Bow was in it, putting up the sail to catch the breeze and gliding across the lake. Bow waved as they disappeared from sight in the distance. The sky changed colour and the clouds parted. A gold light came down and touched the water and two gold orbs went up into the gold light. Then a nun in a blue habit that had a red cross on it and a white headdress appeared. EH, one of the healers that came to our block of flats to give healing to the residents, thought she was one of my Spirit guides. I'd seen her at last! Great!

19 February 2005

Awareness circle again began with the usual prayers. Another guided meditation. We had to visualise a balloon and blow it up, then tie a piece of string around the end to keep it inflated. We then released it up into the atmosphere. I watched it rise up and out of sight. Then I saw a clump of bright red peonies on the ground. As I watched, one of the flowers opened right up and a fairy flew out and rose up into the sky. Then the scene changed and I saw a line of gypsy caravans passing by with their horses and belongings. It was dusk, so they formed a circle and lit a fire in the centre. I was aware of a man dressed as a cavalier riding with them on a big white horse.

He had long red hair and a beard, knee-high length riding boots, knee breeches, a frilly shirt, cloak and a wide-brimmed hat that had feathers in the band. He stood opposite me across the circle. It was a lively scene, with a girl dancing around the fire and a man playing a fiddle, a juggler and two young men engaged in mock fighting with knives. Dogs and children were playing around the parked caravans. GH said that she thought that the cavalier was there to draw me into the circle, rather then for me to be on the outside looking in.

For the psychometry part of the evening, I had taken in my grandmother's blue butterfly pendant from a necklace. AG picked it up and was able to relate various periods of my life – all were true. She also said that after all the pain and suffering I had had, I had gone a long way in healing myself. I was happy to hear that I had achieved so much, as it backed up how much better I had been feeling of late.

It was an enjoyable evening and I was able to relate that there was gypsy ancestry on my father's side of the family, which had originated from Ireland as horse traders, though that was a long while before my grandmother's time.

28 February 2004

We went down to the communal lounge for one of the fortnightly healing sessions that DH and EH conducted. I was last to receive healing, and as I settled down and went into meditation, I saw a rose on a windowsill. It was red and opened up in the sunlight. As it opened a fairy flew out and her movement blew the loose petals around me in a swirling mass. The fairy began to collect up the blown petals, and I joined her as we went up into the sky, putting the petals into a bowl. She wore a cap of rose petals, and her bodice and skirt were also layered with rose petals. Her wings were the colours of the rainbow. Her hair was the golden colour of corn.

I went higher in the sky leaving the fairy behind. Then I saw an angel with a white dress that was edged with gold around the hem and sleeves. I travelled on further and came across several more angels who parted allowing me to see a man on a high-backed chair, a throne, in a blue robe that had long sleeves and a tall hat on his head. The hat was tight fitting over the skull and had a higher part to it reminiscent of a cottage loaf. He was very regal looking with a kind serene face and looked somewhat Asian.

The healing session was over and I returned to normality. A lovely experience!

Another time on a short meditation, I had a row of silver and purple stars coming towards me. In a session with my husband directing healing for my hand, neck and bladder discomforts, I was aware of the man in the brown mac beside me. Just a sideways glimpse of him, then he was gone as fast as he had come.

Occasionally when meditating, I am aware of an out-of-body experience – astral travelling. While sitting in my favourite recliner, I'll go off somewhere and on occasion I'd find myself looking down on my reclining body in the chair. At first you would think that you were dreaming, but it isn't so. In time and when you have gained confidence and experience, you will be able to direct yourself to where ever you wish to be. I believe that the modern term for it is remote viewing.

Another time when I was receiving healing, I found myself looking at a vase of sweet peas. A fairy flew out of a pink one and flew out of the window. I followed it and found myself in a market garden with rows of flowers. The fairy landed on a row of sweet peas and I noticed that there were several more fairies in the flowers. I heard voices and a boy of about six years of age picking the flowers. He had fair curly hair. He gave me a bunch of them and I asked him to smell the flowers. A small girl came forward to show me her flower. It was pink, I admired it and she smiled at me. A tractor came along with a trailer which we all climbed onto, along with the flowers. Another lovely meditation.

Meditation with Helen in our flat, 9 March 2004

We usually started with a prayer and then we went into meditation. I was aware of a church where a funeral was taking place. I followed people walking up a pathway towards the church door. The minister was standing in the doorway speaking to people as they passed him to move into the church. There was a hearse outside the church gates, black horses with plumes on their heads pulling the hearse. It was a Victorian funeral. The people were all dressed in black, as were the children, with black ribbons in their straw hats. There were three farm labourers with string tied around the bottom of their trousers. I saw the funeral begin and some women were wiping the tears from their eyes. The scene changed and I started to rise into the air about to go off somewhere else when Helen called me back to my chair. I then went into another meditation almost immediately.

9 March 2004

Evening meditation in the flat with Reg. I went off and saw some blue irises in a vase on a windowsill. A fairy flew out of one of the irises and out of the window. She was dressed in blue with rainbow wings. I followed her as she flew up into the sky. I then saw two bluebirds and they flew into a tower and I followed them. Inside the tower I had a view of the countryside that was beautiful and saw a big house amongst some trees. I left the tower and went into the house through the French windows, then along the hall and up the stairs into one of the bedrooms. There I saw a woman with the sort of short black wavy hair that was popular in the twenties. She was wearing a leather coat and picked up her gloves and purse. Then she left the room and went down the staircase and out of the front door. I saw a chauffeur open the door of a black car and she got inside. The car went down the drive and along country roads to a train station. The woman got out the car and went into the station waiting room. A steam train arrived and she got into a first class compartment. The scene changed and I found myself in a solicitor's office. The woman with the black hair was sitting in the office with the solicitor. She signed some documents and they shook hands and she then left the office. The solicitor was my Spirit guide. He took his brown mac off the coat rack, put it on, picked up his briefcase and stick and left the office. I spoke to him and asked his name. He replied that it was Rex (or possibly Reg). I asked him if he had a message for me but he did not reply and left.

2 April 2004, Mill Road

H gave the opening prayer. GH led us into meditation with music and it was inspirational – waves on the seashore and the sounds of seabirds. I saw a sailing ship coming into harbour. The sky was red and purple with the setting sun. Stars were beginning to come out in the evening sky. The ship weighed anchor and I saw some activity on deck. Some seamen were preparing to bring cargo overboard into a rowing boat. I watched them wade through shallow water to a sandy beach. They were dressed in clothes of the eighteenth century and were carrying boxes and barrels. There was a young girl, an old man, a tall man and an attractive lady all hurrying to move up the beach at the sandstone steps going up the side of the cliff. At the top of the cliff sat a man on a black horse with a black cloak and a tricorn hat, surveying the scene. As they reached the top of the cliffs there was a cart to load the goods on. Some men moved towards some trees and I saw a church and a house close by. There was a man calling to them to hurry and they took the goods into the church and down some steps to a cellar. I kept well hidden from them. I am sure all was stowed away before long and before the revenue men could find it. GH called us to come back to our seats and all was well.

15 April 2004, Mill Road

We started with an opening prayer. GH led us into meditation. Walking beside a loch I saw a Holly Blue butterfly and followed it into a clearing with a cottage. A lady stood looking over the garden gate and inclined her head as I passed by. I went down a lane, the butterfly ahead of me. It landed on some wild flowers. A young man with a fishing rod and a dog at his heels passed me and I saw some trees, wandered through and saw a clearing with a pool of water. A young girl was paddling in the water and splashing it about her. I sat on a log and watched her for some time. She was at ease and acting entirely naturally. I looked up and saw some fairies flying around in the sunlight that filtered through the trees. One sat on a toadstool watching a butterfly. It was a peaceful scene, listening to the birds singing in the trees and watching the little girl laughing as she played in the water. I moved on up the lane and passed a caravan in the field. Then I saw some crossroads and was unsure which road to take. Then I saw a Spirit guide who was raising his staff and pointing towards me. I think he was going to direct me, but at that time GH called me back to my seat.

29 April 2004, Mill Road

We opened the circle with a prayer as usual. GH led us into meditation. The sun was setting on a beach. There was a wooden chest in the sand, which contained a crystal necklace, book, bottle, pen, paper and another necklace. I chose something from the chest, then moved on. I saw a young girl walking along the seashore who had on a long dress and wore her hair in a knot on top of her head – an attractive young girl – and I gave her the pendant I found in the chest. Then a young man came along and put his arm around her and they walked along the shore, absorbed in each other's company. I walked up the beach to a bank of sand. There was a busy harbour and a boat was being drawn up onto the shore. As I moved on I saw a path that took me away from the sea and so I followed it until I came to some trees. Passing through the trees I saw a waterfall, which was beautiful and I sat looking at the water before moving on. Then I saw a shrine and a holy man. He said 'Namaste' as I passed him by. This was a peaceful place. GH called us back to our seats.

13 May 2004, Mill Road

Jaycee gave us the opening prayer then GH switched on the music to take us into meditation. Imagine a crystal archway – we went through the arch into a cave full of crystals of every colour and size. I chose a green crystal and moved out of the cave. I saw a white light coming down and there was an old man with white hair and a beard. Then on my left I saw a lake and a wide sweep of blue flowers and grass as far as the eye could see. I saw an angel holding the green branch of an olive tree, then GH called us back to our seats.

We then split into groups of three for healing and I was healing AG with GH. GH told me she saw a bridge with fast-flowing water beneath it and said that my eyes would be opened. I enjoyed the evening, especially giving the healing to AG who was drained of energy and felt very tired. Jaycee said she could see a lot of colour around me when I was healing AG.

27 May 2004, Mill Road

JS gave the opening prayer and guided us into meditation. We went up into the branches of a tree, and then took our awareness down into the roots. We were then asked to open each of our chakras and open up to the universe. JS then brought us back and asked each of us to bring the white light down into the heart chakra and hold it there. We were then guided across an ocean to a desert island with a lovely sandy beach with warm water lapping on the shore.

There were seashells, and I dipped my toes in the water, after which we went along a path to a forest. It was cool under the leafy trees. A young leopard was watching me as I walked along the path. I came to a clearing and sat down on a log and I could hear all the birds and monkeys chattering all around me. I picked a flower and put it in my hair. It was cool and peaceful.

I didn't see my Spirit guide on this occasion and came back to my chair and reality.

Coupled with this, we also did some psychometry. We all chose a crystal from Janet's tray and held them for a few moments. Then they were replaced and we had to take one of the others. In turn we gave our feelings, and listening to our inner voices, described what we were experiencing and, if possible, we were encouraged to identify the person who had been holding it originally.

31 May, at home

Helen had loaned us her Bible, and we were chatting about our recent visit to Harry Edwards Sanctuary at Shere, in Hampshire. Helen asked me to link hands with her, so that we were facing each other and so that her guide could come through and hopefully give me some help. I closed my eyes and asked for him to come forward and join us. Reg was sitting nearby, directing his energy to both of us. I became aware of a lot of power coming from Helen into my hands, up my arms and into my body, together with a great deal of green enveloping me, and a sense of knowledge being imparted. Afterwards Helen said that she had never experienced anything like that before. Wow!

The above are just a few examples of what to expect. Your experiences will not be identical to mine, and you will have to interpret them yourselves, perhaps with the help of others in your group. Some symbols and events may not reveal the whole true interpretation at the time, but later on the light might click. Below are some suggested guided meditations.

Inner Sanctuary

Make yourself comfortable in your own space, chair or position. Close your eyes and focus on your breathing. Make it steady, fairly deep and relaxed. Be aware mainly of your outward breath.

Move your awareness away from your breath and up to your heart chakra, adjacent to your physical heart. See within it a small ball of soft light and peace. Place a small replica of yourself sitting in this place and be aware that this is your own specific inner sanctuary. Make it a beautiful room, a wooden shack, a tiny chapel, or a cave on a hillside. Whatever you want it to be. Furnish it, colour it, make it as you like. You are not shut in here; the windows and doors are open and you can see out and beyond to a lovely garden or majestic scenic view. No one can come into this place unless you invite them in. In the distance may be a busy scene, symbolic of the activity of your mind and body, which is continuous. You cannot stop this activity, but you can stand back from it and leave it behind. Observe it and know that eventually you may learn how to influence it. Be at peace. Enjoy the inner sanctuary, relax, let your mind go blank and observe!

Stay in this state for ten, fifteen or twenty minutes. One of your group should stay awake as a controller and guardian. Gradually become aware of yourself, of your breathing, of your hands, feet and physical body. Ground yourself and be aware of the place you are in and those around you.

Discuss your feelings and experiences with others in your group. As you learn to locate your attention at the heart chakra, it increasingly becomes the place from which you can observe others and yourself, and stay calm in the midst of distractions and difficulties and also the place from which you can direct your 'responses'. It is important to learn to be calm in the midst of activity; we are not escaping off to one side! You can focus your attention to this mid-point at any time, not just during your quiet times.

Serenity is not freedom from a storm, but peace amid the storm!

Seashore Meditation

Imagine that you are on a clean sandy beach which is sunny but not too hot. You are standing barefoot on the waterline and the waves are gently washing over your feet and then receding, to and fro.

Gradually, you become aware of your breathing and you time it so that it follows the sequence of the waves. Breathe in and the sea washes in… Breathe out and the waves recede… Your breathing becomes synchronised with the sea. The water has great regenerative power. Imagine this great energy flowing into your feet as you breathe in, flowing up your legs and into your body, arms and head. As you breathe out, release any tensions, anxiety or fear so that it will dissolve into the sea. Each cycle of breathing gives you more energy and greater calmness and you feel free.

Pause for a period of ten, fifteen or twenty minutes as in the previous meditation and return back to your sacred place.

The Medicine Room

This meditation is one that you can do for self-healing. Any problem that you have can be addressed individually, taking one condition, ache, or symptom at a time. The medicine room is filled with little drawers, compartments, bottles or pill holders, each with the name of your personal problem marked on it.

Sit or lie down, close your eyes and breathe deeply three times. Now imagine walking along a corridor until you come across a door that has your name on it. In the lock there is a key. Open the door, enter, close and lock the door behind you. Now look around you. This is your mind space.

You will find the room furnished with shelves and benches. There are two windows overlooking a parkland scene. There is an easy chair, one that you will be comfortable in. This is your pharmacy and your task now is to stock the room with whatever you need.

Ask yourself what is your present need. For example if you are diabetic, find the container labelled 'Diabetic'; if you are suffering from a headache, look for the container marked 'Headache'. There is no limit to the number of marked containers that you might need. Having labelled each one as appropriate you will be able to retrieve the right one each time you need to enter the medicine room. The containers, once labelled, will hold sufficient medication for that particular ailment and it will last the whole of your lifetime.

Select the appropriate container and take one or two of its contents if in tabular form, or whatever amount of spoonfuls, if you have selected a liquid form of medication. Sit back in the easy chair and rest quietly until the problem eases.

Visit your medicine room every day, and certainly whenever you need easement of the dis-ease. (You will notice that I have purposely split the word into two. Most ailments are created because some part of the body is out of balance, and needs to be brought back into alignment with the whole).

Theatre Readings and TV Celebrities

Meanwhile, we were both accepted as probationary healers on Friday afternoons through the Mill Road healing group. We anticipate being fully qualified in the next few months. We were then introduced to a medium who asked us if we would like to work with the angels and ascended masters. We have been working with her help for about a year. We also completed a Melchizedek Ambassadors awakening course under her guidance.

Since joining the churches I have had several readings, the majority written down in a diary and a few of them entered later. Most of them will relate to known friends and family. I have also had the opportunity to meet famous television personality mediums at the Worthing Theatre. The last one was Derek Acorah who was over the other side of the theatre. He asked who Christine was (I didn't answer because I thought there must be more than one Christine in the audience). Then he turned, walked up onto the stage and came down the aisle to me. He asked if he could give me a hug, and then put his arms around me and hugged me close. I had to wash the blouse that I was wearing – twice – to remove his theatre makeup! He went back to the stage and said that I had a huge energy field around me and that my aura was filled with a lot of colour and stars. He said that he had not seen such a colourful one before. He brought through several relatives and a Sister of Mercy, Margaret, (I have a drawing by a psychic artist of her on my bedroom wall) who had been with me since I was a small child. He also told me that I had a lot of work to do for Spirit and that I would write a book. So, here it is! I hope you like it.

After the performance, a woman and her daughter approached me for advice on whom to approach so that her daughter could receive some instruction on spiritual matters, and we suggested that they try and find out the dates and times that their local spiritual churches in Lancing or Shoreham met.

The following day Derek was in a local bookshop signing some of the books that he had had written. We joined the queue and while waiting for our turn several passers-by came up to ask me if I was the lady who had had 'the cuddle'. They had seen it on the big screen in the theatre and had identified me immediately. Several others were doing the nudge-nudge wink-wink thing and I felt as if I was famous, if a bit self-conscious.

Prior to that we saw Tony Stockwell and, although we didn't receive a reading, I was able to chat to him after the show and get his autograph.

Similarly with Sharon Neil. Keith Charles gave us a reading some time ago. It was clear that the message was for us to pass on to a relative. He started off by asking if any one knew a Carol or Caroline. No one answered so he went on to say that this person had died while in an epileptic fit. We were able to take this, but it wasn't a Carol or Caroline, it was a Karen. So you see how important it is that when a message comes through that you are able to identify who the person might be by association with similar names or places. The vibration from Spirit has to be stepped down so much that the mediums sometimes have difficulty in hearing what is being spoken correctly. The rest of Keith's message was really clear and we were able to pass on information to Karen's mother-in-law.

He also made reference to Reg receiving some £500 in the following September. He did, (although it was in October), and it was for insurance money for our residents' association to cover what had been stolen during a break-in the Christmas before. And he was only £22 out! Reg was the treasurer at the time of the reading.

As I have said before, I had seen a Spirit girl at a previous address and where we are currently are living, and I have seen the spirit of an aunt and my cats appear often. The latter we feel on the bed at times, or brushing past us or sitting on our laps. Our daughter Jaycee, who has been seeing Spirit since about the age of four, has seen my grandmother sitting in the bedroom chair, two big black panthers from one of my Egyptian past lives walk through the room, and other spirits and angels around the living room, including a North American Indian with a long headdress down to the floor, standing behind me. Children are also seen. From time to time we know that a lot of activity happens. We are now having circle work in the flat, and we have been told that there is a vortex or doorway in one corner through which Spirit enters. We currently hold physic evenings where experienced people come to sit, and have also had an ascended masters' awareness course held in our flat. Our tutor also holds other awareness classes at her own property, and angel workshops at a local village hall. It surprises me how many new faces we meet, all on the same pathway and with the same interests.

There was an occasion recently where I was confined in our flat for a total of ten days when the lift became inoperative. Although first attended to within the required twenty-four hours, it took the rest of the time to locate the required replacement part. Frustration at being confined is an understatement, and several residents were affected as most of them rely on going out for meals. However, friends came in and with the circle work I didn't totally lose my marbles. On the Friday I couldn't go to give healing, and Reg had to go on his own to keep the numbers up so that no one was let down.

Our family have grown over the years and we currently have eleven grandchildren and six great-grandchildren. One of the latter is a crystal child and one is an indigo child. I did mention earlier in the book that I had a brother who died at a year old. Before our last great-grandchild (Alfie) was born, we had a reading from one of the local mediums at our regular church to say that the brother would shortly return within the family, to the earth plane. I am waiting with baited breath for when Alfie starts talking and responding to see if he has any past life remembrances.

I am really proud of my family now and how they have overcome all of their individual problems, both health-wise and with other matters. The past differences and upsets between us as a family are all forgiven and they rally round us in our late autumn years as far as their own commitments allow. Forgiveness is a big thing and everyone should practise this on a regular basis, not only in forgiving other people, but also themselves. This is a hard thing to understand and even harder to do. One way is to write down all the names of the people that you want to forgive, along with the reasons. Burn the list safely while offering a prayer of thanks and protection not only for you, but also for the people on the list. Send the thoughts back to Spirit with love. You can do this as many times as you feel is right.

Acceptance is another big word! Accept all that is given to you, bad and good alike. What has happened in the previous minute is in the past and no longer need concern you: it can't be changed, but you have the free will to set in motion the next set of circumstances so the bad things can be forgiven and possibly corrected. Think through all thoughts to the end result. Each course of action has a knock-on effect and if not followed through, the unwelcome actions have a knack of returning to you. Accept change. If something has changed, it is the past. Accept the condition.

Rescue Work

At this time of life I am thankful for the love and support of a good husband (a father and companion) and we are in reasonable good health. With the love, support, guidance and help of the Spirit world I will endeavour to walk my pathway in truth and love for the highest good for all.

I would like now to mention my service work with Spirit. I have agreed to work for Lord Kuthumi, in the sleep state, and for an hour every day I do rescue work. I travel in meditation to different parts of the world wherever I'm directed, to rescue children that are trapped in the in-between planes where they might have died suddenly in war, an accident or a natural catastrophe and do not realise that they have passed over. Their ages range from babes in arms up to about six or seven years old. This involves working with the angels who come down in my meditation and help the transition to the higher level.

A great number of the children are from the Victorian era. Some are the children of the rich who come through dressed in beautiful period dress, and I was astonished to see on a TV film I was watching recently that the costumes were, identical to that which I had seen in one rescue period. The film was set in Venice during the sixteenth century and was about a Jewish family that had escaped from Denmark to avoid persecution by the Inquisition. There are also children from the opposite end of the social spectrum such as chimney-sweep boys, flower and match sellers with clothes in rags and no shoes on their feet. Some of the latter were obviously in very poor health, with coughing fits and sores. Several come to me suffering from the trauma that caused their demise, with broken limbs or bits missing.

I must not allow myself to take on the suffering and despair, however, and must keep alert to the fact that they are passing through and that I must not show any great emotion, otherwise my concentration and indeed my own health would suffer. Some come to me with the dark soul of a person who has caused their suffering. I have to demand that they return back to the dark realms until they have acknowledged their own failings and atoned for them and request that they may come forward to the light. Some of the little ones could have been 'captured' for many years without any means of escape.

It's my job to pass the children to the light with a person familiar to them once the angels have brought them forward. Their little faces are a picture. Some are quite anxious, but on seeing the person who has come to meet them, they beam and become all smiles. Babes in arms are usually carried by an angel or occasionally by a person acting on the child's behalf. For each child, a doorway appears, a request for it to open is made, and the child and accompanying person pass through the door into brilliant glorious golden white light and the door closes. On occasions I do not see a door, but rather an escalator, a moving stairway. Now I must emphasise that I do not imagine any of these figures. I am not picturing them in my mind intentionally. They come through on their own as if I was watching a film on the television, and I don't know what the next scene will be.

I feel honoured and humble to have this responsibility, and fervently pray that I can keep working for Spirit in any capacity they want me.

4

Past Life Visions

Here are the experiences that I've had while doing circle work plus others which came to me during my conscious and daytime domestic chores.

During these times I see a lot of my past lives in meditation. In one meditation I was coming out of a wood and was aware that the countryside had changed. I was beside a loch in Scotland. Ahead of me, a man dressed in tartan was standing on a rock waving his tamoshanter in the air. I turned to see who he was waving to and saw the remnants of a bedraggled army. One man was on foot carrying a standard, the rest mostly on foot, with drum and bagpipes. They were all very battle-weary and some were wounded. A lady wearing an ermine coat who was sat atop a white horse rode along beside them. As they passed me I decided to move along with them, and after some time they came to a castle and went through a gate. I looked through the doorway and inside was a banqueting hall and in the middle of the room was a long trestle table, and servants were running to and fro with hot dishes. A man with red hair and beard was standing in front of a roaring fire dressed in a kilt. He seemed to have authority over the servants. In the courtyard a boy was helping the lady get down from her horse. People were running about. A woman was staunching the bleeding on a man's arm (he had lost his hand) and other wounded people were being cared for. I left the scene and went out through the gate into a meadow. Around me was coarse grass, heather and pine trees. It was growing dark and a star appeared amongst the dark clouds and I saw a white light. The light became a lot brighter and I felt myself rise and go into the light. I realised I had witnessed a past life.

Some time afterwards, a friend drew a picture for me while in circle. It was the Scotsman with red hair and beard. She said he was one of my guides. Meg, who I have mentioned previously, told me that she also had the same meditation but on a different occasion, and in it she was the woman staunching the blood of the wounded man. A third person told me she had a similar meditation and identified the tartan as being green with an orange stripe.

In another meditation I was sitting in a cart with other people. I was aware that I was in another time. As we passed along the road, people threw rotten fruit at us and shouted, waving their fists. As we got nearer to the city I could hear a lot of shouting. There were about four people in the cart and when we got into the city I knew where I was from pictures I had seen in books and films. In the middle of the square there was a guillotine with crowds of people shouting and waving their fists and a little lady sitting by the guillotine doing her knitting. As the cart stopped a man came up with a scroll and began reading out names. One of the names was Marie Antoinette and we were her ladies in waiting. She was the first one to die and then we were all beheaded. Then blackness. I felt a pain in the back of my neck for a couple of days after this meditation.

One day, while washing my kitchen floor, I became aware of another scene of a past life as the wet floor became a living picture of life in Roman times. The women were washing garments and bed linen in the open air in a row of stone sinks and then hanging them up to dry. On the other side of the square there were market stalls with people buying and selling items. Animals – chickens and geese – were being sold. Roman soldiers were milling around the crowds. I felt as though I was in a dream as this scene passed before me. When I came out of the trance all was as it should be in this time period and the floor was finished!

I had a meditation in the flat, with Reg as my gatekeeper. I was aware of being with several people who had to keep their activities secret. We met in rooms in dark passages. We belonged to a religious sect called Cathars. We had to be careful and always watch our backs. We lived in dangerous times and I got the feeling that all was not well. There was a lot of muttering going on and we seemed to be going around keeping our heads down in case we were recognised.

There was also another meditation where I was also a Cathar (tolerant Humanists with strong anti-Catholic convictions) in France. I was one of two hundred people led to a plateau where we were all burned at the stake. Being one of the last, I could see all that was being done most horribly before me. At that time others were walled up in caves to die. We have since met several people around Worthing that also identify with the same period. Indeed, one of them said that they were on the side of the Inquisition and responsible for inflicting those terrible deeds.

I had a card reading from a local medium who owns a crystal shop. As she held my hands she told me that many aeons ago, I was in the star group known as Pleiades and that I was a star child. There was no vegetation as we know it, only mountains and water. The mountains are the colour of turquoise; the ground and vegetation appear to have a crystal-like quality about them. The beings there have no bodies and are made of light.

I was sent from there to the Mayan people on earth as an ambassador. But no one would listen to me as I did not have a forceful enough nature and had no previous experience in that position, or sufficient communication skills.

From there I was sent to Egypt. In an Egyptian past life I was a dancer with a middle-class lifestyle. People that I danced before gave me expensive gifts of jewellery. My husband at the time worked at the court of the Pharaoh, but I saw little of him and had my own life and freedom.

Another lifetime saw me as a monk, caring for animals. I was able to give them healing when they were sick or wounded and to me they were more important than people. The order had a vow of silence, so again I wasn't allowed to communicate, a thing that I seem to be carrying forward in several of my lifetimes. I was also another monk in Tibet.

All this changed about a year ago, and I have been told that I am here to help, teach and guide the people of the world when the world changes start to take place.

Reg and I were in the development circle for eighteen months, and in that time we had learned the basics of psychometry, healing and psychic reading. We also attended a few workshops once a month for some nine months with a local medium who was also a tutor. Here we learned flower and colour reading, sand reading, chakra meditative breathing and aura reading. At another meeting a psychic artist drew a picture of an Indian girl whose name was North Wind. She was given as a guide for me.

Evidence of Survival of the Spirit

The Spirit lives on when we die. Our physical body is but a shell and carries the Spirit while 'alive', so that Spirit can experience the trials and tribulations of living while in the material plane. All mediums give us this evidence of survival from the messages of those that have passed over.

Readings from Mediums and their Interpretations

Here are a few of the readings that I have received from the platform at various churches. Not all are entered as they mainly deal with family members and would not mean anything to the reader. They are purely examples to show that messages do come across from Spirit and are not body language or mind readings.

Following the reading we note how we interpreted what was given. It is a good idea when first starting out to keep a diary of events such as experiences while doing meditations, and what is given in readings from mediums.

8 June 2003, taken by JC

This was the very first reading. The medium said to me, 'I have your mother's sister here, a small woman with short hair and a twittering nervous manner. She sends her love and says she is your guardian and watching over you. She has a country garden and tends the flowers including some tall blue ones. She never married and passed suddenly. Dorothy! Do you remember the card games for pennies?'

Alice is named and Margaret is here (expressed as Marge or similar).

Interpretation

This is Auntie Dolly (born Alice Hilda) who did love flowers and for several weeks before first attending the church I'd had an inclination to buy some delphiniums for indoor decorations.

Dorothy, (thought to be Doff – another aunt in this instance) is the proper name for Dolly. Doff did play cards with friends and Bernard, her husband's soldier friends.

Alice was thought to be Auntie Alice, one of the Greens from Angmering, but could have been validation for Auntie Dolly, whose real name was Alice Hilda.

Dolly was a spinster and did die suddenly on her way to Tuesday lunch in a cold, snow-laden February.

Marge was interpreted as Margery Beaton, our dear friend from Yeovil.

22 June 2003, taken by RW

'I have a father figure here,' the medium said to Reg. 'He looks like you and says that you have your mother's mannerisms. He says he is proud of the way you have conducted your life and identifies that you have always done things yourself without calling for help from other people. Another man is here and he wants to thank you for helping him to pass over.'

Interpretation

This is Reg's dad and yes, Reg is like his mother in a lot of ways. As the family know, he has got on and accepted his life and done things on his own. He felt very humbled by this message.

The second person is identified as my dad who went to hospital too late for corrective surgery. The hospital conducted tests over a week and barely fed him. I believe he initially died while Reg, Ilsa, and I were there. The staff stabilised him and he eventually fully passed over at 4.30 a.m. the following morning with his son Alan at his bedside.

28 June 2003, taken by JH

Addressed to me: 'I have a lady with white hair and I'm feeling a choking sensation as if I can't breathe. She wishes to thank you for helping her pass over. Also a father figure who is putting his arms around you and saying that he loves you very much and sorry that he did not do this in life. Also, a Violet and Winifred.

'Do you know Len? He is still causing havoc as he did in life with his joking and mucking about.'

Interpretation

To me: The woman was thought to be Marge again and the thanks should go to Jaycee our daughter as we had asked her to contact Marge while in a coma. Jaycee said that contact was made and she suggested to Marge 'stop mucking about and make up your mind which way you want to go.'

George (Dad) obviously sorry for the split between Mum and himself and was apologising for not being around to give his love and support. Violet and Winifred could not be identified at this time.

Len was my mother-in-law's brother, Reg's uncle. This was unexpected and visibly shook Reg; tears welled up in his eyes.

6 July 2003, taken by VG

The medium addressed us both: 'I see a bright green/blue light over both of you. This indicates either you are healers or receiving healing.'

Validation

I had received the first of six sessions of spiritual healing in Grafton Road church the previous Wednesday 2 July.

27 July 2003, taken by GT

A somewhat erratic reading that touched on both of us.

'Do you dream?' the medium asked Reg. He answered in the affirmative but said he could not remember them. The medium asked me the same question and I had the same reply, but then I remembered the recurring dream I had before my accident of a large expanse of windows, flames and smoke.

'There are thanks from Spirit for thanking a young child and a father figure is giving you a single red rose for his love.

'Do you know Pat?' (asked of Reg).

GT first came to a chap halfway down the congregation and asked if he knew a sailor. Then GT asked another chap if he knew a military man with a leg wound caused in the war.

Interpretation

The sailor was present in the Spirit world and meant nothing to either man in the congregation. GT identified a military figure with a leg wound from the last war but who did not die from that wound.

Reg put his hand up and said George was a sailor, not a soldier, although he was a gunner on the ship. He had shrapnel from the wartime, and suffered from leg ulcers in his leg until the metal was finally removed during his last twelve months on earth.

The windows in my dream were later identified as those of Yeovil Hospital and related to my accident. The young child was thought to be Joanne, one of my granddaughters, when she was a baby and I'd had to call a doctor. The rose was from George.

There are three Pats who could be identified: one a cousin and the other two workmates, but none of these could be fully identified by the reading.

5 August 2003, taken by RH

This reading stands out from the norm and is one that Reg had. It concerns his brother whom he had not heard from in some time.

'Can anyone take a Dougal?' the medium asked.

'Yes,' said Reg.

'I'm not sure whether he has passed over or not as he is coming to me through the centre of my back. If they come through on one side they have definitely gone over, but if they're on the other side they are still on the earth plane. So I'm not sure about this one.'

'Dougal is my brother's nickname,' said Reg, 'and he's only called that by his friends. The family only call him Doug or Douglas. I could understand the confusion as I hadn't heard from him for some fifteen years and he has had several operations that could give you the impression of him not being totally here.'

The outcome of this was that in talking to a member of the congregation that had Internet access, I was supplied with four likely phone numbers. One was Doug's and we are now in regular contact again.

Synchronicity

Through life's pathways, events can happen that make you wonder if they were pre-ordained or destined to happen. One event may not mean anything at all, but when you piece all the parts of the puzzle together, things that have happened over a period of time, they eventually make sense. For instance, have you ever met someone, or visited somewhere that led you to meet an acquaintance, who in turn has resulted in you meeting yet another person, which again led to someone else?

Here are some stories to illustrate what I mean, including another which identifies how future events can be sensed before they happen, even if you are unsure of exactly *how* they will happen.

Back in the early 1950s a sailor in his early teens went on board HMS *Illustrious* for a couple of weeks during his initial training to familiarise himself with life on board ship for the first time. He had left home to join the forces and did not have a girlfriend at the time. Like all young servicemen in those times he decided that he would put a pin-up in his locker. Most of the ones available were sketches similar to the type that the American airmen used to paint on the front of their bombers, a curvaceous figure of a girl in a swimming costume or sarong, and the men would give her a name.

This sailor found a sketch that he liked, one of a blonde, blue-eyed girl kneeling down and with a gorgeous smile. Her arms were above her head sweeping her curls up. She was kneeling in such a manner that you couldn't see her legs below the knees. The name the sailor decided to give her was 'Chris'. On leaving the ship, the poster pin-up somehow got left behind and was forgotten until some twelve years later.

My husband Reg was that young sailor, and the picture that he had is how I am now – only much older – but according to him I still have gorgeous blue eyes, 'blonde' hair (although it's helped a bit these days) and a lovely smile!

A young girl somewhere in North America decided that she wanted to save up for a bicycle. She ran errands and got herself a paper round and managed over a period of time to save nearly enough for the bike. At school one day, the teacher told the story of a boy down in Columbia who was very ill and desperately wanted a bike so that he would have something to look forward to which might enable him to get better. The young girl took all her savings to the school and added it to the collection. Feeling more sorry for the boy than herself, she felt that his need was greater than hers. A few years went by and she attended college where she made friends with another girl. An invite to tea at the friend's house was arranged and she duly went. There she met the friend's brother and they got chatting. The boy's mother went on to say that when they were in Columbia the boy had been very ill and some school in North America had donated a decent-sized amount of money, which enabled them...

Here our original girl interjected and said 'Don't tell me, you bought a bike!'

This story was told some twenty years after the girl and the boy were married, and they have had a happy life.

During his service life of some ten years, Reg has told me that on several occasions during his time at different naval air stations around the country, synchronicity occurred. Whenever an 'incident' was likely to happen, work would come to standstill just prior to the event. The air and ground crews would down tools and come out of the hangars around the airfield waiting for the 'something' to happen. They never knew what, nor had any messages been sent to the various offices, and no crash crew alarms had yet been sounded. They just knew!

This happened only when someone or something was in imminent danger, so inevitably there were several eyewitnesses to a crash whenever one occurred on the airfield, and at no other time.

The same thing happened on the day of my accident. Reg was strapping the pilot into an aircraft for the next lot that were to take off, when both stopped and the pilot stood up saying that they were to wait a bit! Others around the work areas had also stopped. Something was about to happen! Two planes were taxiing for take-off. They both took off in tandem (one beside the other with one slightly in front). The slipstream of the leader caused the one behind to stall, and it crashed into my caravan. The leading plane continued its flight.

Ian Taylor, a medium from Lewisham told this next story to the congregation of Worthing Spiritualist Church. He has given me permission to repeat it here the best that I can remember it.

He had just finished a service somewhere and was on his way home when he suddenly decided that he would go for a pint. Not something he did very often, but on this occasion felt that it would relax him for the evening. While at the bar, a very large gentleman came in, the size of the proverbial brick outhouse, with a determined expression on his face as if looking for trouble. As he sidled up to Ian, the latter turned to him and said, 'You're from Yorkshire and your mother goes to a spiritualist church!' The man spluttered, his jaw fell open and he was obviously shaken to the core. During the resultant conversation, it turned out that the man had recently come down to London, would have nothing to do with spiritualism while up north and had silently prayed that while down south he was determined to find some evidence of spirituality without going to a church to get it. Both Ian and the man had been led to the same place at the same time!

Missing Out

Another title could be 'Coping' or 'What I can do and what I can't do.' The things that I couldn't do after the accident were and still are, emotional rather than physical. The physical I can get round one way or another, but of course there are exceptions!

No, I cannot walk far; yes, I had to have my two sticks, when younger, to totter around; yes, I needed an arm to help me get up kerbstones or a couple of steps; and yes, I now need more assistance when out and about, and even going to the loo these days is difficult, particularly if the floors are slippery, or there aren't any wall bars. Not all conveniences have adequate wheelchair turning room.

No, I can't carry shopping; no, I can't open swing doors on my own; and no, I can't reach the things on the top shelves in the supermarkets, or the lower things in the freezer compartments.

Around the house, if I am on the floor without my pins, I cannot reach the upper cupboards. Similarly, if I am standing in the kitchen leaning against the worktops, I cannot reach the bottom cupboards or pick anything up off the floor.

Most clothes shops these days clutter up the aisles with racks of clothing so things either get knocked off the rails or get run over with the chair, despite the fact that they are now breaking the law.

Visiting the family is also a problem, as one house has shingle running up to the front door and another has six massive steps. All have upstairs loos, so any visits are of a short duration, which they sometimes seem to react to. Even going on holiday can be awkward, either for available space in the room or dining room. Sometimes, the space in lifts is inadequate. Dipping my toes in the sand and paddling at the water's edge? Not on! I couldn't even get down to the beach to play with the kids or make sand castles. Walks in the woods are again a no-no; also walks along the downs are sorely missed. I'm constantly frustrated!

In the early days school visits for parent/teacher consultations sometimes proved to be out of the question. Again it was a case of there not being enough room to manipulate the chair, or the teachers being on different floors of the school.

No, it's not a 'poor me' situation for there are others who have even more distressing tales to tell. I will just ask you to re-read the preface at the front of the book. It's a wake-up call to try and make you aware of the problems that others may have. Physical problems can be accepted and are. It's the emotional feelings that one has to come to terms with and accept. It's taken me many years to learn this fact and now that I have opened up to Spirit I am happy again and face my lot with fortitude.

I ask that you now look at those around you, either at home or when out and about, and look with your eyes and hearts open. How do others cope? What problems on a daily basis do they have? Open your hearts and send them loving thoughts. The more people that do this small thing, the better the world will become. And give them a smile!

You could also give them help and healing!

5

Degrees of Spirit, and the Energy Levels in which they Reside

There is the life force, which can be affected by thought and prayer, and is in every living cell.

There is the essence that can be contacted by mediums. The thoughts and energies of those departed from this life, for another existence. They are more commonly called 'the dead', but to my mind if someone is dead then surely they cannot be contacted for two-way conversation or thought transference.

The ability to pick up vibrations from an inanimate object (psychometry) is not quite the same thing. This is the historical memory vibration. What or who is contacted is the ongoing living energy in another dimension or vibration.

Think of the lifecycle of a dragonfly. In its early life it goes around in the muddy murkiness of a pond, living, feeding and growing. When the time is right, according to its growth programming, it climbs out of the pond onto a plant stem and climbs out of its grub-like shell and turns into a dragonfly. How much like an angel is that? We climb out of the murk of the earth plane and ascend to the realm above in all its glory and brilliance!

A model of this energy is represented by the emblem on the front cover, and is explained in the section entitled The Encircled Cross and Star.

There are the energies known as the ascended masters. These appear in human form, and can contact your mind/awareness, direct. Other energies include the Buddhas and enlightened ones, some of the latter being on the earth today.

There are the celestial galactic beings that come from other planets on the far side of our galaxy and from even more distant galaxies, which appear in many different forms. These are the stuff from which some science fiction is made, but much truth is spoken in jest! There are training schools around that give instruction on the beings and energies of other worlds, for example, the Pleiades and Melchizadek.

Meanwhile, back on the planet earth, there are the groups of people who work with the earth energies and those that repair or formulate new earth grids and lay lines, in order to try and stabilise the earth energies.

Spirit i: The Intangible

I have talked about mediums, readings, visions and past life experiences, but what is Spirit?

It is the essence that surrounds us all. It is the 'thing' in between the very molecules and stuff that we are made of. It is everywhere. It is the vibration of life, is the force that makes the seasons and allows the seeds to germinate. Recent laboratory experiments show that thought can manipulate the very cells of our being and one person has even photographed molecules of water that are on the point of freezing, that have had words directed at them, both via thought and the written word (see *The Hidden Messages in Water* by Masaru Emoto). The results are amazing.

Write down the words 'love' and 'gratitude'. Place the written word around your water jug in the fridge and notice the difference in taste after a short while; compare it with the taste of water straight from the tap. You could place your hands around a glass of water, direct loving thoughts or offer up a prayer of thanks and still notice the difference. It would be even more convincing if you were to have a group of friends around and try the experiments blind (inasmuch as they had not seen what you had done to the jug or glasses of water before they arrived).

The photos of the crystallized water previously mentioned were also made with negative thoughts directed at the water. The results of these showed that the water had been affected in not a pleasant way, as the images have ugly patterns, instead of pleasing patterns as shown on those that had positive, loving thoughts directed at them.

What had made the changes? Scientists are currently evaluating DNA and gene changes. It was thought that DNA and genes paved the way in which we evolve, but now the opposite is happening and they believe that it is our day-to-day, even minute-to-minute thoughts that actually change the direction of activity towards one result or another. Take, for example, people that have had miraculous cures by believing that they could heal themselves, by mentally refusing the growth or illness within them. There have even been cures that have been affected over a distance, as happens with absent healing. A group, any group of like-minded people can sit together quietly, calm their thoughts and concentrate on the person that needs some healing activity, wishing and praying that the person being thought of has their complaint removed. This can also be done individually.

If you can, imagine that the healing process starts at the cellular level, whereby the very cells of the organ, muscle, ligament, skeletal bone or blood cell are reduced to one particular atom. Then concentrate on that part receiving healing thoughts. The thoughts can then be directed to adjacent cells and you can visualise the healing process expanding and growing. Alternatively, one can visualise a growth reducing in size until it disappears.

One method that can be used is not so much to ask for the person to be healed, but for the reason for the condition to be healed. If the reason for the condition is removed then the complaint as a whole will be cured.

As an example, our great-granddaughter has had a condition from birth (she is now seven years old). Recently she started to eat everything – and I mean anything – even bits of fluff and minute pieces of carpet. This resulted in her not holding any food down and when the hospital eventually gave her a scan, they found a large hairball in her stomach. The decision was made to operate, and a date was set. Knowing of her problem, we included her in the weekly prayers at the healing group, entered her name in a few books designated for those that needed healing and, of course, placed her on our daily prayer list. Her mother also conducted hands-on healing. When the surgeons operated, they were astounded to find that there was no sign of the hairball. It had gone completely. It was also established that it hadn't passed from her body naturally. The time scale from when first diagnosed through to the operation was something like three weeks!

With several people involved in the prayers, each person will have their own way of directing the prayer and each in their own words. No one prayer will be identical to another, and it would be doubtful if any two used the same thoughts or words. Offer the thought/prayer to Spirit and they will do whatever is necessary for the highest good. Such is the power of prayer.

All items are made of atoms, and depending on their vibration rate, made up of solid, liquid, or gaseous elements. Even stones and mountains are comprised of movement within their structure, so nothing is in a static mode. Thought, if powerful and concentrated enough, can and does change the invisible world around us. If loving and harmonious thoughts were directed to the people with whom you have disagreements, you will notice a change in their manner and way of thinking. If this could be directed to the leaders of men, think what changes could be made to bring the nations and religions together. For this to happen we all need to recognise that acceptance is a powerful force. Accept other people's religions and doctrines rather than trying to change them; accept the difficulties and hardships that come to you – they are part of the learning curve. It is also some of the hard knocks in life that open you up to spirituality. It's the jolt to the very core of your being, be it physical, mental or emotional, or perhaps all three; an illness, coupled with circumstance, or else the people you meet or the locality that you move to.

With acceptance, it would be just as well to offer up thoughts of gratitude. Be thankful for what you have, for there are those around you that are not so well off. I don't mean material things – they are not of spirit and you can't take them with you when you pass over. Rather, think of well-being, outlook, health, abilities, and disposition to others. The last powerful word is forgiveness, not only for others, but also for yourself. I have given some guidance on how to deal with this previously, so I'll just let you contemplate this one.

Spirit ii: Identified and Recognised by Mediums

Another definition of Spirit is the one referred to by mediums. Clairvoyants are able see Spirit; clairsentience is the ability to sense a spirit and clairaudience is the ability to hear Spirit. Some mediums can receive one or all three of the above. Others have the ability to go into trance and the voice of Spirit can be heard directly.

This is the vibration that exists between this world and the next. To the energy that our dear departed ones transmute to and can result in messages being passed from the invisible world to this. Usually the first responses include verification of who is making contact by describing the person in spirit, or by some mannerism that they might have. You may be told of some specific action that only you would know about. Of course names, anniversaries, and place names are also concrete evidence.

It is at this level that you might see, hear or sense some communication when you start meditating, although you might also be able to see mythological creatures and the spirit of the earth energies, such as elves and fairies.

Spirit iii: The Collective

Several treatises liken the spirit as being the individual facets of a diamond. There is the whole diamond, referring to a larger group of spirits, with the smaller shining surfaces relating to one person, i.e. one facet is equal to one person. I prefer to liken Spirit to being an ocean, all the oceans of the world joining together, say. The oceans have rivers going into them. These have tributaries that are fed by streams and tiny rivulets. The water is made of drops that sparkle and shine in the sunlight, duplicating the facets of the diamond. However, the drops originated from the sky as rain that in turn had been evaporated from the oceans. So, to my mind, the Spirit that is within us is more like the drop of water that returns to source at the end of its natural cycle. Each droplet is unique in that it might be carrying different particles of matter and in different proportions to any other, as we are – individual and unique.

Food for Thought

Give some thought to the word 'sacrifice'. Not the killing of live beings to appease the gods, but more the action that occurs naturally and in many walks of life. For example, the sun gives out heat and light, sacrificing itself for the benefit of the earth. It heats up the seas, which in turn sacrifice the moisture that rises as clouds. These in turn sacrifice themselves so that rain falls and feeds the planet and plants. The soil gives up nutrients to the plants and the plants give us food. Farmers give up time to make the harvest and the drivers give their time to deliver the goods to the shops. So it is with everything: somewhere along the line someone or something is giving up, sacrificing, for the benefit of others, again affecting change. What allows the changes to happen? Spirit!

Food Blessing

'For what we are about to receive, may the Lord make us truly thankful'. Surely it's up to us to be thankful to the Lord, not that He should make us thankful?

One blessing that my husband says is: 'Bless all that has made sacrifice to bring this food before us. Bless the food and pray that in its eating and digesting it is converted to the highest good. I thank Spirit for all the blessings given us this day.'

Collective Prayer

As individuals and as groups we pray for peace on earth. This we have, but only in small pockets around the globe. We get what we ask for! Rethink the request before it is offered as a prayer. Ensure that the thing that you pray for is complete in all its ramifications, and accurate down to the last detail. What you send out is what you will receive; ponder again on the pond and the pebble.

The Lord's Prayer

How many of you say this without really thinking about the words? Say it again, slowly and concentrate on what is being said.

Is it grammatically correct? Do you really mean what you are saying?

Take for instance the phrase 'Deliver us from evil'. You have free will, so in reality it is *you* who choose to do the evil! It is not up to the Lord to do the delivering! Now try replacing those words with '*Protect* us from evil'. Similarly with the phrase 'Lead us not into temptation'. I suggest that this ought to be 'Leave us not when in temptation'. It's only my interpretation in this day and age. I do not mind if you disagree.

As prayer has the power to accomplish miracles, what a great idea it would be if instead of standing silently with your own thoughts when we are called to keep a minute or two of silence for some catastrophe that might have occurred, where we think of those that had passed over or to think of those left behind, we all followed a standard prayer, said either aloud or silently, in unison. Perhaps with the media being used to voice the prayer said by all nations, in all languages, and in all time zones around the world. The leaders of all the churches, religions and faiths need to utter the same prayer aloud so that the people of all nations could follow it at the same time and not silently to themselves. What power that would create!

This is my suggestion for such a prayer:

'To all nations, creeds and peoples of the world. We gather here to offer hope and healing to all that have suffered. Hope to the living and to the disembodied spirits that do not know where they are. Hope to the rescuers who are searching and hope to the relatives of those that are lost.

'Healing to those in anguish, in pain and injured. Healing to those that are giving aid to the living and the dead. May all accept the situation and be led to do the best that they can for the highest good.

'May forgiveness be asked for and given to the perpetrators of atrocities and ask that they will be shown the error of their ways, that they do not receive as they have given out and that they in turn can seek forgiveness.

'The natural events that turn the very earth upside down and the waters of the earth that flood the land, cause considerable anguish for us, the peoples of the world. We implore that future events are gentle, that the earth turns or disrupts gently, or that the floodwaters rise slowly, giving us the opportunity to remove ourselves safely from the areas to be affected.

'We need the leaders of the world to be of one mind, to strive for worldwide peace and not argue on the rights or wrongs of another's belief; to facilitate the even distribution of food; to provide life-giving clean water; to sustain and make healthy all those in famine and drought stricken areas.

'We all need to accept and have tolerance of the beliefs of others, without question. The religions of the world are all rooted in the same basic doctrine, so help us to accept those beliefs in principle, not to fight against them. If we do, we are fighting against our own beliefs.

'May all that is done be done for the greater highest good, to preserve this dear beloved planet, the peoples, animals and minerals and the very structure of the earth.

'May we learn to think as one for the common good, that the vibrations of the earth are raised so that sensible, right-thinking communication can ensue for the good of all.'

6

The Spiritual Hierarchy of the Angelic Kingdoms

For some time now I have been aware of angels around me. They appear in my flat while I am doing my rescue work, they appear when I'm saying my prayers, during meditation and when I am giving healing.

They come peacefully with a soft and gentle approach, and instil in me a sense of calm and confidence. They are shining and beautiful! You can call on them at any time when you are stressed, in despair or simply whenever you feel in need of help from above. They will guide you in whatever walk of life you are in, whatever job that you do, whether it be in education, in the medical profession (either as practitioner or patient), in industry or government... The list is endless. They will help you to make decisions and guide you. The secret is to listen to the first thing that is said by your inner voice and accept it without question. Once you start to try to analyse the response you may come unstuck as the logical and analytic part of the brain kicks in.

They are always around us, so whenever you are in need just ask for their help and you will receive.

Below are listed the names of the 'unseen' forces who help us in our everyday lives. If the plea is heartfelt and sincere without a harmful thought, they will come to you at any time. The angels have different names according to their attributes which depend on their individual level. They are listed in ascending order. Many books are available which identify them from the highest order downwards, (in deference to the higher beings) which can lead to confusion if you have just started to see or contact them when you meditate and are on the bottom rung of the ladder, so to speak, but particularly if you are on the angelic path. Occasionally

you may be fortunate to make contact direct with one of the
higher beings in your early days. So in this instance I have started
the list in reverse order, at the bottom rung of the ladder.

Third Sphere: Heavenly Messengers

This sphere is sometimes called the Third Triad.

Angels

The angels are the beings who work most closely with humanity
and nature. Each person has a guardian angel. There are an
infinite number of angels that are available for healing, illumi-
nation, creativity, nature, music, dance, writing, literature,
protection, emotions, politics, science, technology, peace, art,
relationships, purity, ceremonial order and magic. They cover all
aspects of life, including that in all the manifestations of nature. If
you invoke them with sincerity, they are happy to come to you
providing the plea is for the highest good.

They are the workers under the direction of the archangels.

Archangels

These are of a higher rank than the angels and in some schools of
thought are believed to serve larger areas of human existence.
Each archangel has a female counterpart and govern, or appear, on
a different ray. Each ray has a different associated colour:

Ray One:

Michael and Faith

Royal purple

Protector to give us strength and courage to change the nega-
tivity within us into positive aspects of love and peace, and to
help clear ourselves of limitations.

Ray Two:

Jophiel and Christine

Dark pink

Helps to find divine light and wisdom within. Encourages us to become a clear and open vessel for enlightenment.

Ray Three:

Chamuel and Charity

Pale green

Gives us the power of adoration through the higher mind (self). They help us to awaken our own self-love, and thereby find or see divine love in all and everything.

Ray Four:

Gabriel and Hope

Copper

These pertain to the Grail Cup and of Resurrection and Ascension. Are the voice of God and will illuminate the soul from the higher realms of Spirit. Awaken our remembrance of purpose and destiny.

Ray Five:

Raphael and Mother Mary

Emerald green

Archangels of healing for the earth and all its creation. They purify and facilitate physical, mental and emotional healing. They help us to love our bodies and experience unconditional love.

Ray Six:

Uriel and Aurora

Pale yellow

Of ministration. Will assist us to overcome our worst disappointments and turn them into blessings of faith and inspiration. In moments of despair they help us to discover our own truth and be in a 'state of Grace'.

Ray Seven:

Zadkiel and Amethyst

Dark blue

Holds the power of invocation and prayer. Through the glory of the violet ray will transmute our lower natures into the gold of our higher selves. We can become a glorious alchemist of light.

Principalities

These are of a higher rank than the archangels. They are the guardians of large groups such as cities, nations, and multinational corporations. It is said that one of these beings holds in its heart the love for a unified global order for planet earth.

Second Sphere: Heavenly Governors, Guardians of the Universe

Sometimes called the Second Triad.

Powers

There are the protectors of the universe. These fight and protect against the evil activities of fallen angels and demons, and it is their ceaseless efforts that help to ensure that all of the other angelic beings can fulfil their duties lovingly and with success.

They are the bearers of conscience, and are the keepers of the collective history of earth.

The angels of birth and death are part of this group. These beings are able to draw down the energy of the divine plan for earth, which enables humanity to perceive and understand the interconnectiveness of all things.

Virtues

These bestow grace and courage to humans, and have the ability to perform miracles. They are able to send out considerable quantities of divine energy and virtuous qualities to humanity on earth.

Dominions

These beings are often depicted carrying golden orbs or sceptres as an indication of their authority. They regulate and govern the work of the angelic beings. They also help to integrate and blend the materialistic and spiritual worlds.

They do not have many contacts with individual souls on the earth plane. They could be called the divine bureaucrats.

First Sphere: Heavenly Counsellors, Pure Light

Also known as the First Triad. These are angelic beings of the highest order and they never descend to earth.

Thrones

This is the lowest level of the highest sphere of angels, also known as the Ophanim and also called the Wheels. Ancient mystics have described them as 'fiery coals'. They are the heavenly companions and counsellors of all the planets.

Cherubim

These being work above the Thrones and are the guardians of the light throughout the universe. Since historical times they have been depicted as cute little cupids rather than the most majestic beings that they really are, being second in line to the highest being in the celestial hierarchy. It is seldom that they make personal contact with beings on the earth plane. It has been said that they are involved in the keeping of the celestial records.

They also work with the Sanobim who work as helpers and assistants to the highest level in the First Triad, and Cherubim have the opportunity and potential for advancement to become Seraphim. They usually work in pairs and with the Sanobim are the most efficient workers on all of the planets throughout the universe. They do not serve as attending angels to humans.

Seraphim

The highest order in the celestial hierarchy. They are physically described as being of pure light and thought. They are the regulators of the movements of the heavens and surround the throne of God. They have untold responsibilities in God's administration of the infinite universe.

There are twelve master Seraphim working with the supervision of planet earth:

1. Epochal angels are entrusted with the overseeing and directions of the affairs of each generation and root race.

2. Progress angels are entrusted with the task of initiating the evolutionary process of successive social ages. They help the progress and development of evolutionary creatures.

3. Religious guardians – angels of all of the churches.

4. National life angels are directors of political performance in earth life. They are involved in international relations.

5. Angels of the races work for the conservation of evolutionary races, regardless of religious or political affiliations.

6. Angels of the future forecast and predict the future of the galaxies and are thus the makers of future eras.

7. Angels of enlightenment are in charge of planetary education as well as mental and moral training as it concerns individuals, family groups, schools and communities within nations and races.

8. Health angels – the angelic healing corporation.

9. The home seraphim are dedicated to the preservation and advancement of the home, the basic needs for shelter of human civilisation.

10. Industry angels are a group concerned with fostering industrial development and improving the general economic conditions for the peoples of the earth.

11. Angels of diversion are responsible for the fostering of the leisure activities for the peoples of the earth.

12. Superhuman ministers are the angels of the angels. They are assigned to minister all other superhuman life on the planet.

Life and Death

These have no set time scales – each will vary depending on the advancement of each individual soul and what they are required to contribute towards the greater good.

Life

Life as we know it is the conscious part of ourselves that can react to thought processes. It is our awareness, and governs the period from when we are born until we die. A life span may be only a few hours, ten years or even of some three score years and ten, but in the general scale of things our time here is only miniscule.

Death

This is where we cease to exist in the material world. We have stopped breathing and are what is known as 'brain-dead'. We are but an empty shell. Think back to the carcass of the dragonfly insect that has climbed out of the murky water, left its shell behind and become a glorious dragonfly, or the empty shell that is left behind when a chick is hatched. It is instantaneous; one second there is life of some kind, then, when the accepted view of consciousness has stopped, there is nothing! Or is there?

Life after Life

The consciousness of Spirit continues to exist, and this is the one that mediums connect with. It is also the level of vibration where we can enter the Halls of Knowledge to gain further insight into spiritual matters or to further our quest for additional information and learning.

Depending on your personal development in this and previous lives, you may choose to stay at this level for further experiences and lessons.

Life before Life.

Now here's a thought! This is where Spirit goes full circle. It is the period immediately preceding birth and a new life. When conditions are right in the Spirit world, a soul may decide to return to earth for additional experiences, or to enable others to learn a lesson, not one of retribution but one where they may have to learn new skills. Perhaps a soul wishes to awaken the thought processes of someone who has lacked compassion and caring for others, in which case it is a lesson of love, humility and motivated by a general desire to help mankind in whatever way they can.

From life before life you need to cross the river of forgetfulness and, as far as you are aware, forget all that has gone on before. You forget that time you were in Spirit before you were born. You forget the past life experiences and you become aware of whom you are and grow again in the new material world. You will not remember the promises you made to yourself before being conceived and reborn. The memories are tucked away deep in your subconscious self. It is within your soul and can only be reawakened by the way you choose to live. You can liken the river of forgetfulness to the time you were in the waters of your mother's womb.

Imagine a circle with a tail coming out of one side. Part of the circle can be entitled 'Life' another section, 'Life after Life', a third 'Life before Birth'; the circle can then be bisected with a tiny mark 'Life', indicating when 'Death' occurs, somewhere after 'Life as we know it'. The tail could be called the 'River of Forgetfulness'.

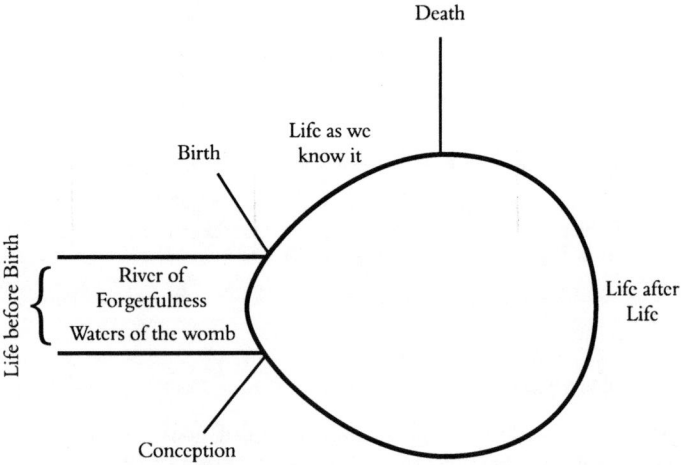

There are now many television programmes that show some individuals who do remember previous lives and previous incarnations. There are also those who have undergone past life regression, sometimes more commonly known now as 'soul retrieval' and who have experienced the happenings of a different era. One or the other – or both – are proof that the ancient theories are true!

Of course, the best proof is for you to personally have 'an experience'. To the sceptic no proof is enough; to a believer, no proof is necessary!

Karma

The saying 'As you sow, so shall you reap' is the simplest way of putting down the results of thoughts and actions.

A great deal can be said about karma and there are many doctrines and books on the subject.

All you have to do (and it is not so simple as it sounds) is think before you act or speak. Look for the end result, the long-term effect.

If, for example, you have harsh words with someone, they might repeat those words to a friend or relative. The original message will be altered, and much harm will be done; others may come and have words with you directly, or someone might take it into their heads to do you physical harm. Your family and friends will then hear your side of the story and decide on some form of retribution. Isn't this how wars start between relatives, friends, neighbours, and even countries?

A relative or friend is killed in a car accident. Anger and frustration ensues. The living face untold difficulties, be they financial, care or transport problems. The anger and frustration does not have an end result. You have to adjust to the circumstances and accept what is.

The earth is acting out karma. We extract the minerals and oils out of the ground. What happens? Without the natural elements in the ground, the earth plates move in an unnatural way, resulting in earthquakes, probably before the cosmic timescale desired it to be so. We chop down the trees of the forests, which results in a change to the balance of oxygen in our environment. This changes the world-wide weather patterns... The list is endless.

All the forced movement of mankind may have caused the economic problems around the world, where whole nations were transported in the past, for the financial benefit of a few.

It may be that you or your kin are experiencing repeated problems of genetic or other hereditary problems carried over from previous lifetimes, or perhaps a poverty or hunger issue needs to be dealt with, or even one caused by those that had too much materially. There is often a lesson to be learnt, either for those who have to carry the burden, or for those around them that have to learn to be able to accept or deal with the problem. If there are excessive amounts of material things, then they should be used wisely for the benefit of others.

Again, think of the pebble in the pond and how the waves come back to the original point and beyond. The good as well as the negative thoughts and deeds have a similar action and reaction, which emphasises the meaning of 'as you sow, so shall you reap'.

There are meditations and instruction CDs that can help with the release of karma, both from this life and the far distant past.

7

A String of Pearls

Here a few poems that I have accumulated and I apologise to the originators. These came into my possession, one at a time, from various sources and without any reference to the authors, with the exception of 'Starlight' by Tiffany, a member of my circle.

Guardian Angel

I am a tiny angel,
I'm smaller than your thumb,
I live in people's pockets,
That's where I have all the fun.

I don't suppose you've seen me,
I'm too tiny to detect,
Though I'm with you all the time,
I doubt we've ever met.

Before I was an angel
I was a fairy in a flower;
God Himself hand-picked me,
And gave me angel power.

Now God has many angels,
That He trains in angel pools,
We become His eyes, and ears, and hands,
We become His special tools.

And because God is so busy,
With way too much to do,
He said that my assignment
Is to keep close watch on you.

When He tucked me in your pocket
He blessed you with angel care,
Then told me never leave you,
And I vowed always to be there.

I am your guardian angel.

Great Spirit

Great Spirit of light, of love,
Of peace and harmony,
Teach us, we pray thee, to hold
The flame of our spirit so
Sheltered within our hearts
That it may burn serenely
Unflickering in the winds of
Circumstance.
So may our souls be calm pools
Where truth is mirrored.
So may our minds be poised,
Clear channels for the work of
The Enlightened ones.
So may the light shine in the hearts of all
Men for ever.

I Am Special

[Now this one is for you, reader!]

I am special...
In all the world there's nobody else like me.
Since the beginning of time,
There has never been another person exactly like me.
Nobody has my smile.
Nobody has my eyes, my nose,
My hair, my hands, or my voice.
I am special...
No one can be found who has my handwriting.

Nobody anywhere has my tastes
For food, music or art.
No one sees things the same as I do.
In all of time, there's no one who laughs like me,
No one who cries like me;
And what makes me laugh and cry
Will never provoke identical laughter
And tears from anybody else, ever.
No one reacts to any situation just as I would react...
I'm special!

I'm the only one in all creation
Who has my set of abilities.
Oh yes, there will always be someone
Who is better at one of the things I am good at,
But no one in the universe can reach
The quality of my combination of talents,
Ideas, abilities and feelings.

Like a room full of musical instruments,
Some may excel alone,

But no one can match the symphony sound
When all are played together.

I am a symphony.

Through all eternity no one will ever look,
Talk, walk, think or do things like me.
I am special...

I am rare.

And in all rarity there is great value.
Because of my great rare value,
I need not attempt to imitate others;
I will accept – yes, 'celebrate' my differences.

I am special, and I am beginning to realise
It's no accident that I am special.
I am beginning to see that God made me special
For a very special purpose.
He must have a job for me
That no one else can do as well as I.
Out of all the billions of applicants,
Only one is qualified.
Only one has the right combination of what it takes.

That one is me...

Because...

I am special.

Starlight

Look at the stars and how they shine
Look at their beauty they're so divine.
They're shining brightly in the sky,
If you try, you can fly as high!

Tiffany

Hugs

It's wondrous what a hug can do.
A hug can cheer you when you're blue.
A hug can say, 'I love you so'
Or, 'Gee! I hate to see you go.'

A hug is 'Welcome back again!'
And 'Great to see you!'
Or, 'Where've you been?'
A hug can sooth a small child's pain
And bring a rainbow after rain.

The hug! There's no doubt about it:
We scarcely could survive without it.
A hug delights and warms and charms;
It must be why God gave us arms!

Hugs are great for fathers and mothers,
Sweet for sisters, swell for brothers.
And chances are some favourite arms
Love them more than potted plants.

Kittens crave them, puppies love them,
Heads of state are not above them.
A hug can break the language barrier
And make the dullest day seem merrier.

No need to worry about the store of them,
The more you give the more there are of them.
So stretch your arms without delay
And give someone a hug today!

What is Peace?

Peace does not mean glorious sunshine and cheer
From the moment that a day may begin.
Peace is the power that comes to the soul
When the light of God shineth in.

Peace is the joy that God ever giveth
And the quietness that He imports.
Peace is the strength and the courage He gives
To vision, bodies and hearts.

Peace is hushed prayer and receiving the answer
In submission and quietness too.
Peace is new hope for tomorrow
And the promise of new joy to you.

One Touch of Beauty

One touch of beauty, one shimmering thing
Like a butterfly's wing
Can open my heart to the day.
One edge of sky
Soft silver-grey
One almost blooming flower.
Look at the light on a leaf, the delicate tracings
The frail interlacings
Of sun and of shadow.
Watch the crystal snowflake fall
Silent and small, magnificent.
Open your face to the sky and the stars,
To the towering faraway hills,
Pause while your soul
Fills with beautiful music.
Walk on the diamond-flecked sands by the sea.
Look at a field with bright golden rod,
Touch hands with beauty touch hands with God.

An Angel Prayer

Dear angel ever at my side,
How lovely you must be,
To leave your home in heaven
To guard a child like me.

When I'm far away from home
Or maybe hard at play,
I know you will protect me from
Harm along the way.

Your beautiful and shining face,
I see not, though you are near,
The sweetness of your lovely voice,
I cannot really hear.

When I pray, you're praying too,
Your prayer is just for me.
But when I sleep you never do;
You're watching over me.

Prayer to your Guardian Angel

Guardian angel
Guard me from harm.
Protect me in sleep
Without cause for alarm.
Keep me safe through the
Darkness of the night,
And wake me gently with
God's morning light.

Epilogue

I was inspired to write this book as I felt there is much to say about life, its trials and tribulations and how one can find a solution to them. I could have written chapters on crystals and chakras, but there are plenty of books already written on these subjects, and I recommend that you find the ones that are right for you. Suffice to say that while the earth energies are changing, the body energy centres are moving: the higher chakras are coming down and entering the physical body, with the lower ones descending to Mother Earth. This is the reason so many of you are feeling light-headed and spaced out and sometimes feel as if you are in dreamland (without any artificial help!)

Being at the end of my life, I believe that I have some authority to be able to comment on how one's thought pattern might help others, although my mothers' advanced age suggests that I still have another twenty years left. If I were called now, I wouldn't really mind as I am ready and my bags are packed!

Perhaps within these few pages you might find the answers or inspiration to enable you to seek Spirit. Your God. Open your mind and your heart. Think within as you read, listen to your inner voice, and find the path that you want to tread.

I quoted Matthew 10:26 at the beginning of this book, and I would now like you to ponder on the next two verses:

> What I tell you in the darkness, *that* speak ye in light: and what ye hear in the ear, *that* preach ye upon the housetops. And fear them not which kill the body, but are not able to kill the soul: but rather fear him which is able to destroy both soul and body in hell.
>
> Matthew 10:27–8

In all meditations or when working with Spirit, *remember to give yourself proper protection.*

I could say that this is the end, but it isn't... It is the beginning of the rest of your life. Use it well and with good intent.

God Bless!

Printed in the United Kingdom
by Lightning Source UK Ltd.
136058UK00001B/49-63/A